Dancing with God

Dancing with God

Anglican Christianity and the
Practice of Hope

JAY EMERSON JOHNSON

morehouse

Morehouse Publishing, P.O. Box 1321, Harrisburg, PA 17105

Morehouse Publishing, The Tower Building, 11 York Road, London SE1 7NX

Morehouse Publishing is a Continuum imprint.

Cover art: Cinco Banistas by Antunez, Kactus Foto, Santiago, Chile/SuperStock

Cover design: Wesley Hoke

Library of Congress Cataloging-in-Publication Data
Johnson, Jay Emerson.
   Dancing with God: Anglican Christianity and the practice of hope / Jay Emerson Johnson.
      p. cm.
Includes bibliographical references.
ISBN 0-8192-2112-0
1. Anglican Communion—Doctrines. I. Title.
BX5005.J62 2005
230'.3—dc22
                                    2004016397
Printed in the United States of America

05 06 07 08 09 10   10 9 8 7 6 5 4 3 2 1

For all the "sheep" at the
Church of the Good Shepherd
in Berkeley, California

To all belongs the dance on high,
For the one who does not dance,
does not know what is coming to pass.

–From "The Hymn to Christ" in *The Acts of John*,
New Testament Apocrypha (second century)

Tomorrow shall be my dancing day,
I would my true love did so chance
To see the legend of my play,
To call my true love to my dance:

Sing, oh! my love, oh! my love, my love, my love,
This I have done for my true love.

—A nineteenth-century carol by William Sandys

I danced in the morning
When the world was begun
And I danced in the moon
And the stars and the sun
And I came down from heaven
And I danced on the earth—
At Bethlehem I had my birth.

Dance then wherever you may be,
I am the Lord of the Dance, said he,
And I'll lead you all, wherever you may be
And I'll lead you all in the dance, said he.

—A twentieth-century carol by Sydney Carter

~ Contents ~

Acknowledgments ix

Preface xi

Introduction: The Priest and the Disc Jockey 1

1 ~ Waltzing the Two-Step: A Hopeful Theological Method 21

2 ~ The Dance Floor: An Invitation to Courageous Faith 41

3 ~ Hearing the Music: The Trinitarian Rhythms of Christian Faith . . 61

4 ~ Holy Hula Hoops: Jesus and the Hope for Human Thriving . . . 85

5 ~ The Tango: A Spirituality of Divine Seduction 111

6 ~ The Virginia Reel: Visions of Unrealized Communion 131

Prospects for the Dance:
Hopeful Wallflowers and Postmodern Anglicans 153

Notes 173

~ Acknowledgments ~

Some of the ideas in this book first saw the light of day in two series of lectures I was invited to offer at Grace Cathedral in San Francisco—the first in June 2002, and the second in January 2003. I am grateful to the Reverend Mark Ruyak for the invitation and to those who attended the lectures. Their willingness to engage in lively conversation and ask astute questions contributed to the shape of this book.

More generally, the approach I take with respect to Anglican theologies and traditions was tested and refined by the students and the faculty colleagues with whom I worked at the Church Divinity School of the Pacific in Berkeley, California. The Graduate Theological Union, of which CDSP is a member school, continues to offer a stimulating and creative context in which to "do theology," and I am profoundly grateful for what I learned and continue to learn there.

I could not do any of this work apart from the sustaining nurture of the Church of the Good Shepherd, also in Berkeley. Those "sheep" restored my sense of what a loving Christian community can and should be, and they continue to incarnate the rich potential in Anglican styles of Christianity.

I am also grateful to a friend and colleague, L. William Countryman. Among other things, Bill is one of the sheep at Good Shepherd, which means I have the privilege of hearing him preach on a regular basis and learning anew on those occasions how the Bible can be read faithfully and intelligently and as a matter of genuinely good news. Whenever I had doubts about this project, Bill kept encouraging me to write. I'm thankful for those conversations with Bill as reminders of how to "do" theology in particularly Anglican ways.

Debra Farrington, a friend and my editor at Morehouse, took a chance on this book after reading only the introduction and first chapter, which gave me the energy to keep writing. I can only trust the rest of it strikes her as worth the risk she took on a new author. Taking that risk is what I would call the practice of hope, and I'm grateful for it and to her.

~ Preface ~

The image of "dancing with God" may seem like an odd one for a book on Christian theology, perhaps even more so for a book dealing with Anglican theologies. More than a few people probably assume dancing and theology have at least this much in common: Other people do them. We watch professional dancers at the ballet or at a ballroom dancing competition on television and never dream we could be so graceful and skilled with our bodies. We might pray now and then, attend church, and share opinions about the liturgy, but theology often seems remote and restricted to professionals—to teachers, academics, or clergy.

The good news of Christian faith suggests something different: Each and every one of us is invited to dance with God. Each of us can dance. Each of us can do theology. The invitation is extended to all.

I came to this realization by becoming an Anglican Christian. I don't mean the concept of dancing and my own desire to dance better convinced me to join the Episcopal Church, which I did many years ago in a small, Midwestern, Anglo-Catholic congregation. Yet over time, as Anglican traditions fostered dynamic and expansive ways to practice Christian faith, my life as an Anglican seemed to take on the fluid and graceful qualities associated with a dance.

I believe this image of dancing with God can tease out some fresh ways of talking about Anglican Christianity, especially today in the dizzying complexities and increasing anxieties of a twenty-first-century world. Such a world, of course, demands more than fiddling with questions of Anglican identity. The challenges of deeply entrenched mechanisms of fear and bigotry and of poverty and violence require more from us than debating what it means to be an Anglican. Still, such debates can prove quite fruitful if they lead to a deeper exploration of the good news of Christian faith and how to put that faith into practice for the sake of human flourishing. Anglican traditions offer an opportunity to do precisely that, to revitalize Christian theology among those who yearn for lively intersections between their faith and the societies and cultures in which they live.

These aspirations spring from my own quest, stretching over a number of years now, to integrate my love of dancing and my love of God. For quite some time I understood these two loves as distinct spheres in my life, not necessarily at odds with each other, but neatly separated. Seeing how deeply they're connected and richly intertwined prompted a moment of conversion for me, a deepening of my faith. This book is the product of reflecting on that connection and its implications for appropriating the Christian gospel as truly good news, which, for a host of reasons, no longer seems an obvious way of speaking about Christianity.

I worry, for example, that the crude caricatures of Christian faith in American popular culture, whether in television and film or in media reporting, have rendered Christianity flat, static, and two-dimensional. The concept of Divine Reality suffers from these flattened images: I fear they have caused far too many to have missed God's invitation to dance. I also worry that the increasing disillusionment with religious institutions in Western society—for which there are many good reasons—can trigger a dismissal of Christian traditions on a much wider scale. I am likewise troubled by the kind of formulaic and moralistic presentations of Christianity in tracts or "how-to" pamphlets or among some television evangelists. These create an impression of Christianity as either one option among many for self-improvement or as a rule-based system for buttressing cultural mores. God's great dance of life certainly offers more than that—at least one would hope so.

Anglican styles of Christian faith invite us to move beyond moralisms and platitudes and into a more deeply textured encounter with Divine Reality. While many Anglican Christians lament the perpetual lack of precision in defining what Anglicanism really is, this imprecision can create breathing space for sorting through what it means to be a Christian at all, for discovering anew why Christianity is a religion of good news. Anglican traditions broaden the "dance floor," so to speak, on which to practice and experiment with Christian faith. These fluid and dynamic qualities in Christian believing and Christian living lead rather naturally to the image of dancing. Rather than a system of theological thought or a program of religious discipline, I want to suggest ways of talking about Anglican Christianity primarily as an invitation to dance.

The image of dancing in religious contexts is certainly not new. It appears throughout the long and varied history of Christian spirituality and in the spiritual practices of many other religious traditions. Dancing also occurs in many other social contexts and not just for explicitly religious purposes. As far as we know, human beings have always danced, and for a wide array of reasons—to express joy, for romantic seduction, as a form of social protest, to create communal cohesion, establish friendship or the bonds of love, as a work of art, or simply for fun, as an expression of the fullness of life. All of these reasons to dance play a role in this book as a way to describe encounters with Divine Reality and how such encounters invite us to live. They also describe how Anglican traditions can foster, encourage, and nurture those encounters for the sake of putting the good news of Christian faith into practice.

The goal here, however, isn't so much to become better Anglicans. That kind of project would imply the existence of a blueprint for a final product, as if we could one day say that we have completed the work of religious formation. Anglican theologies, with all their ambiguity, diverse styles, and peculiar mosaics of historical traditions, invite us to understand Christian faith and theology as perpetually unfinished. They invite us to expect new insights, to discover and revise misconceptions, and to welcome the gifts offered by even the most unlikely sources. So rather than striving to become the quintessential Anglican, which today means widely different things to different people, Anglican theologies invite us to put Christian faith into practice even without a precise blueprint or perfect clarity of vision. The long and diverse history of Christian traditions suggests exactly that kind of approach: God invites us to "do" Christian faith as best we can, even when our understanding is muddled or our belief has faltered. The same thing can be said about dancing.

Some types of dancing require instruction. Jazz, ballroom, and country-and-western line dancing, to name a few, all depend on carefully choreographed steps. Other types of dancing encourage a more relaxed choreography and free-form improvisation. In either case, it takes some courage to move away from the margins and out onto the dance floor. When we do, even after extensive instruction, there's no guarantee we'll dance flawlessly or correctly or even gracefully. Yet the music invites us to dance nonetheless. Taking those first steps to the music is what I would call the "practice of hope," which comes with no assurances of "getting it right." So we dance with hope, pausing when we need to for some further instruction. The same thing can be said about Christian theology.

I harbor no illusions here of crafting a definitive expression of either Anglican Christianity or Christian faith generally. I don't believe a neatly packaged religious faith is possible or even desirable. My more modest aim is to suggest some ways to think about Anglican traditions as inspiring the practice of hope, which I do believe Christian faith is all about. By the end of this book, I will be more than happy if the image of dancing with God seems perfectly natural to you, especially if you practice your Christian faith as an Anglican.

INTRODUCTION
~ The Priest and the Disc Jockey ~

Christian faith and dancing belong together. The bond they enjoy in the history of Christian traditions and spirituality appears in a variety of biblical stories, liturgical forms of worship, in poetry, spiritual songs, and hymns, and in theological ideas themselves. Even though this bond is deeply forged and appears in a wide range of religious traditions, the link between dancing and God would not have occurred to me in the context of my quasi-fundamentalist childhood religion. While the link did not automatically appear after I joined the Episcopal Church as a young adult, I was nevertheless delighted to discover that religious people do indeed dance to have a good time, or least for a good cause. I came to that realization by attending my first "Episcopal Charities Ball" shortly after being confirmed as an Episcopalian.

Beyond charity balls and the occasional Mardi Gras sock hop, the link between dancing and ideas about God appears most often when Christians celebrate a wedding. Such an occasion clearly calls for a bodily expression of joy for which only a dance will suffice. Yet I do wonder about the extent to which a typical wedding party recognizes the connection between the "religious" portion of the celebration, which transpires in a church building, and the dancing, which happens at a rented hall or country club. As the newly-wed couple and their guests leave the church, pile into their cars, and drive to the reception, the distance between religion and dancing grows with every passing mile.

American popular culture tends to perpetuate this pattern, especially in films and on television. According to the typical Hollywood version of a wedding, only after the religious rite unfolds in staid and formal gestures do we see the happy couple kicking up their heels at a safe distance from the church. If we see the priest at all after the ceremony, he (rarely she on film) looks slightly uncomfortable and out of place in the midst of all the revelry. My own experience as a parish priest certainly followed this cultural pattern. Planning and presiding over weddings accounted for a significant portion of my time in a suburban Chicago parish, especially during the summer months. I soon came to see the extent to which couples and families divide these celebrations into two distinct spheres. The first is presided over by the priest; the second, by the disc jockey. The priest worries about the religious ritual while the disc jockey orchestrates the party. Almost without fail, my parishioners expressed surprise whenever I asked the bride to dance at the reception—delighted surprise, to be sure, but surprise nonetheless. I suspect their surprise came from the image of an officially religious person, dressed in a clerical collar, dancing. Those experiences taught me something important about my own naïveté as a newly ordained person and contemporary cultural assumptions about religion: The image of a priest or a minister having a good time takes people by surprise.

Like dancing, the image of a wedding also enjoys a long history of rich spiritual and religious associations, whether in the parables of Jesus or in the romantic and even erotic images running throughout the writings of mystics and Christian poets. Over time, these deep connections weakened as the cultural assumptions of modern Western societies widened the gap between what most people think of as "religious" and contemporary definitions of the strictly "secular." For many people today, religion refers to a private realm of serious if not esoteric belief neatly roped off from the arena of "real life"— where we throw parties and have a good time. While relatively few Christians today would object to dancing at a wedding reception, more than a few miss the connection between the dancing and the ceremony that preceded it: The religious rite itself points to, and is actually an instance of, God's great dance of life.

Bridging the gap between dancing and Christian faith involves much more than what transpires during wedding liturgies. A religious celebration of marriage points well beyond the couple exchanging vows and toward a broader insight for the life of faith. As with any romantic relationship, theology begins with desire. Celebrating romantic desire and the commitment of love, as weddings properly do, points to this deeper and more fundamental dynamic in encounters with Divine Reality to which the long and varied history of Christian traditions bears witness. Simply put, God desires us, and with a desire no less intense or erotic than the desire we see displayed during a wedding.

Reflecting on God's desire, let alone the possibility that God might find me desirable, played virtually no role in the pattern of my early faith development. I believed the burden of my relationship with God fell squarely on me, on my own desire, will, and commitment. I suspect many other Christians have experienced something similar in their own lives of faith. For me, trying to be the "best little boy in the world," I hoped not merely to please my parents: I wanted desperately to get God's attention. I don't mean I was simply taking my experience of stern parents and projecting that experience onto God. In fact, my parents were far from stern. My earliest memories of them are of happy and loving people quite willing to indulge their only child. Yet somehow I came to think of God as a remote figure and mostly detached from our day-to-day lives. The exception, of course, occurred when mistakes were made, or what I learned to call "sin." While I clearly understood God as loving and forgiving, it did not occur to me to that God hopes that I, one of God's own creatures, would thrive and be happy. I certainly did not imagine that God might desire me or invite me to dance.

To say not only that God loves us but also that God desires us is to give voice to one of the most fundamental aspects of reality. Tragically, religious institutions tend to bury this good news under layers of regulations, policy debates, political machinations, and, frankly, dull books. Religious communities constantly face the temptation to codify and institutionalize their faith, and Christianity has always run the risk of being reduced to texts, whether in the form of scripture, creeds, or liturgies. Most Christians probably know or at least suspect that there is more to religious faith than reading ancient texts. I wonder if teenagers realize this when we send them off to a Confirmation class to learn the Catechism. To be sure, Christians, just like Jews and Muslims, are "people of the book," yet we rarely stop to consider that we are also "people of the dance." Sadly, even more rare is the idea that we are people of God's own desire.

The flat and rather static portrayals of Christian faith so many have inherited today stand in stark contrast to the dynamic image of dancing with God, with the God who actively invites us into the great dance of life. Historically, theological traditions encourage this more dynamic view, which offers fresh ways to speak about Christianity as good news, and from such speaking, to live a life marked by loving reconciliation and hopeful justice making.

I stumbled upon this more dynamic approach to theology as I tried to discern what it means to practice my faith as an Anglican Christian. Some ineffable quality in Anglican sensibilities encouraged me to engage in the business of Christian faith as something like an adventure, full of both surprise and risk, and which is not quite finished yet. This book is an attempt to articulate that experience with the hope of inviting others into its orbit. For me, it probably helped that I was not born into Anglican Christianity but instead adopted it by choice. This doesn't mean I made a thoroughly informed choice, or that I knew exactly what I was doing. I won't say it was a rash decision, the religious version of impulse buying. It was more like being seduced and falling in love rather than following a carefully designed plan.

When I first stepped foot into the Episcopal Church, an Anglo-Catholic parish of "smells and bells," it felt slightly exotic to my Midwestern Bible Belt sensibilities. At the same time, it also felt like coming home, even though I couldn't explain it to my bewildered friends and family, who came mostly from Baptist or "free church" traditions. I suspect many others who were religiously something else before joining the Episcopal Church could describe a similar experience. This book grew out of that experience of finding Anglican styles of Christian faith attractive and wondering why they continue to energize my life and relationships.

In many ways, some of them quite subtle, Anglican Christianity invites fundamental inquiry into the meaning of religious faith. The typical lack of precision in defining Anglican identity creates a broad religious space in which to examine Christian faith more generally. To be sure, this doesn't immediately sound like good news. Human beings generally seek rules, instructions, and systems for organizing our lives. We rely on owners' manuals for our cars, instruction booklets for our VCRs, and "how-to" books for our spiritualities. Those who expect something similar from Anglican forms of Christianity are quickly disappointed. Pausing to recover from such disillusionment can create a rich opportunity. For those of us who left traditions with more restrictive parameters, the relative breadth of Anglican traditions offers some breathing space for discerning what it means to be a Christian at all, and whether or not Christianity itself creates a place we can call home. I suspect this is part of the gift Anglican Christians offer to the wider Church; it has certainly been true for me.

Negotiating the diversity of approaches to Christian faith within a single congregation, much less the worldwide Anglican Communion, requires a healthy scrutiny of assumptions. (And religious people, no less than any others, tend to operate from a staggering number of unexamined assumptions.) By embracing the rather peculiar world of Anglican Christianity, I learned to read the Bible in new ways, examine theological traditions with fresh questions, and pay closer attention to the religious experiences of the communities in which I have lived and worked, including two Episcopal seminaries and several congregations. Juggling these various aspects of Christian faith in Anglican contexts has felt less like constructing a religious system from carefully crafted texts and more like a dance.

The image of dancing would surely inject some fresh energy and even new insights into what it means to live with the kind of Anglican diversity so evident in many congregations today and even more so in the worldwide Anglican Communion. Dancing can provide a useful metaphor for practicing a fluid and dynamic vision of Christian unity. There is, however, much more at stake with this image. Dancing with God offers a way to talk about Christian theology itself and to energize the practice of Christian faith with genuinely good news. And the good news we wish to speak and to live has much more in common with dancing during a wedding reception than many theological books and sermons would lead us to believe.

To be clear, I don't wish to disparage texts or to discount the importance of creeds and liturgies. To the contrary, I actually love books. My house is literally overflowing with them, and I consult them frequently for preaching, teaching, and liturgical design. I continually consult the texts of Christian traditions for clues and insights into what it means to live my life as a beloved and cherished child of a dancing God. Indeed, these many texts provide a vital link to the history of human encounters with Divine Reality, and there is still much to learn from that history.

Still, there is surely more to religious faith than studying texts, just as there is more to a marriage than reading books on wedding planning. Religious faith reduces to learning texts in about the same way dancing reduces to waxing and polishing a dance floor. We know there is more to dancing than that. We know there is more to marriage than a beautifully performed wedding. Do we know the same thing about theology and our lives of faith? We have tragically missed the point of Christian faith if we fail to see in all the texts and creeds and liturgies of Christian traditions the invitation to dance with God, to dance with the God of abundant life who so eagerly and long-ingly desires us.

As with any marriage, a wedding marks only the beginning of a relation-ship that will take many turns and present a host of life-changing opportu-nities and quandaries. Dancing at the reception gives only a foretaste of the kind of dance still to come, not to mention the hard work required to sus-tain a relationship over time. So while some probably worry that the image of dancing implies excessive sentimentality or that it romanticizes the seri-ous business of theology, professional dancers know this is simply not the case. Principal dancers, the corps de ballet, Broadway stars, and chorus members continually receive instruction, practice skills, seek guidance, try new techniques, study the classics, and generally work hard to improve their craft and their art. The dance of faith is no different.

Encounters with Divine Reality and the implications these encounters carry for our lives and our relationships are rarely obvious and plain. They require scrutiny. They demand further study and careful evaluation within a community of the committed faithful to discern what they mean for us and for how we live. That's the work of theology. Even when we feel at home in a particular religious tradition, we seek to understand its inner logic and why it should beckon us as it does. For Anglican Christians, this kind of scrutiny of a religious tradition presents a serious challenge.

SEARCHING FOR AN ANGLICAN IDENTITY

Some of the more profound aspects of human life resist precise definitions—what it feels like to fall in love, or to hold a newborn baby, or to stand for the first time on the edge of the Grand Canyon. Words often fail us when we try to communicate these experiences to others. "Well," we finally say, "you just had to be there." We have similar difficulties in describing what we mean by "good art," or a "great movie," or a "perfect sunset." After many attempts to define what these things are, many of us finally say, "Well, I know it when I see it." The same thing has often been said about Anglican Christianity.

When pushed into a corner to define their tradition, more than a few Anglican Christians find themselves stammering, struggling to give a precise definition for a loosely collected set of traditions and procedures that they know defies precision. They also suspect this imprecision is part of what they find attractive about Anglican styles of Christian faith. Still, these fuzzy edges of Anglican Christianity can cause some chagrin in a world that values exactitude, clarity of vision, and fine categorical distinctions. As the diversity of the Anglican Communion now takes new turns and as the process of globalization grants nearly immediate access to differences and disagreements, can we still say about Anglican Christianity today that we "know it when we see it"?

The sixteenth-century birth of the Church of England, initiated by King Henry VIII and given more palatable shape several monarchs later by Elizabeth I, launched a strange-looking Christian community. It was not quite Protestant, like the reformers in Germany and Switzerland. But it was not quite Catholic, either, like the Pope, who refused to grant Henry's request for a divorce, or like the Spanish, whose armada threatened England's shores during Elizabeth's reign. Anglican Christianity emerged as somehow both Protestant and Catholic yet not quite either one. These historical points of contact for Anglican styles of Christian faith were virtually unknown to me when I was introduced to the Episcopal Church as a college freshman.

I grew up in the Evangelical Free Church, yet another church body notoriously difficult to define precisely (I vaguely recall its roots reaching back to opposition to Swedish Lutheranism in the nineteenth century). After a steady childhood diet of austere church buildings and lecture-like sermons, I was quickly intrigued by the highly stylized worship of a small Anglo-Catholic parish. That congregation's life together looked like my childhood fantasies of medieval Catholicism, but they prayed without any reference to Rome. I decided to leap first and look later, quickly immersing myself in parish life, which felt rather daring. The tradition in which I had grown up ingrained in me a deep suspicion of anything resembling Catholic piety. Many of my friends, especially those I had met at the private Christian college I was attending, voiced concern and occasional alarm about my newfound religious affiliation. This simply fueled my resolve. In the context of my Midwestern, upper-middle-class Evangelicalism, joining the Episcopal Church felt like late-adolescent rebellion.

Thankfully, I made this denominational shift for more substantive reasons as well. The rector in my new religious home preached the gospel, which reassured my Evangelical sensibilities, and the liturgy drew from ancient traditions, speaking to a Catholic heart I hadn't realized I possessed. Within a year I presented myself for the rite of Confirmation; two years after that I embarked on the process toward ordination. To say I made a leap, in other words, is putting it mildly.

Still, even as I was leaping, I took time now and then to look. I became familiar with the early political history of the Church of England (usually marked by the succession of monarchs from Henry VIII to Edward VI, Mary Tudor, and Elizabeth I). I read about some of the classic shapers of Anglican theological traditions (most commonly identified as Thomas Cranmer and Richard Hooker, but also later figures like F. D. Maurice and William Temple), and I learned as much as I could about the structure and rites of the Book of Common Prayer. In seminary, I studied the aftermath of the American Revolution and the factors leading to the emergence of the "Protestant Episcopal Church of the United States of America." The religious chaos among American Anglicans created by George Washington's victory marked the beginning of the Anglican Communion, a loosely affiliated network of national provinces with each one in some sense independent yet nevertheless "in communion" with the Archbishop of Canterbury in England.

Throughout these historical and theological excursions, my confidence remained strong that I would eventually uncover a definitive expression of what it means to be an Anglican. I felt certain this search for Anglican identity would bear some recognizable fruit. After all, Roman Catholics can turn to the Pope or at least to the Vatican for a sense of communal identity and religious cohesion. Presbyterians can turn to the Westminster Confession and Lutherans to the Augsburg Confession. Members of my family who belong to Baptist traditions insist on simply turning to the Bible. Anglicans can turn to, well, what exactly?

Early on in seminary, I learned some of the standard answers to that question. Anglican Christians turn to a three-part theological method based on scripture, tradition, and reason, often referred to as the "three-legged stool," with each leg equally balanced against the other two. But don't other Christian traditions do the same thing? Some Methodists I know insist that Charles Wesley invented it.

Anglicans also turn to the Book of Common Prayer as both the symbolic and liturgical basis of our unity. But many of the provinces of the Anglican Communion have long since abandoned the 1662 version of that book, adopting their own versions of those rites. And besides, don't Roman Catholics and Lutherans, among others, turn to similar texts?

Anglicans have likewise turned to the image of the *via media*, the middle way between the extremes of either Roman Catholicism or Protestantism, as a way to describe our peculiar style of Christian faith. But this hardly stakes out a distinctive theological position, and it quickly turns rather soft and shapeless as Anglicans appear unwilling finally to take a stand on anything. Catholicism without the Pope or Protestantism without biblical literalism certainly creates a large and open dance floor, but can it tell us how to dance?

After serving as a parish priest for three years, I returned to graduate school and embarked on a doctoral program in philosophical theology. I had no pressing interest in studying "Anglican theology," convinced by then that no such thing exists. And of that I am still convinced today. If by "Anglican theology" we mean a set of definitive texts, creeds, and historical documents that sets Anglicans apart from other Christian bodies, we will search in vain to find it. We can, however, find a wide array of theologies being done by Anglicans. And there is a difference. Noting how Anglicans do theology may prove more fruitful than detailing what Anglicans believe. This doesn't mean Anglican Christianity has no theological content. To the contrary, Anglicans actually do hold some strong theological convictions. Yet these convictions emerge as a function of how we go about the business of putting our faith into practice, of how we manage to dance, both with God and with each other.[1]

The fluid character of Anglican Christianity continually provokes controversy, as any diocesan convention in the Episcopal Church amply demonstrates. How Anglicans struggle through such controversies offers an important insight into Christian faith more generally. Rather than a set of propositions to which we give our assent, Christian faith is something we hammer out, struggle with, knead like clay, sweat over, and, thankfully, dance to as we hear music we have always longed to hear. It won't be handed to us in a biblical text. We won't find it preserved for us in a historical creed or in a diocesan resolution. It won't suddenly emerge in a perfectly crafted liturgy. All of these are important tools, without which our faith would be greatly impoverished, if not impossible to practice. Nevertheless, they are tools, and like every tool, they are designed for use, for actually doing something as we continue to journey, stumble, dance, and trip our way into what Jesus called the "kingdom of God."

In short, we may not know Anglican styles of Christianity when we see them, but we will know them as we do them over time. Trusting the "doing"

6 even when we can't see the goal of our faith with perfect clarity, good deal of courage. It will inevitably create moments of upheaval and instability along the way, and more than a few theological loose ends: An individual Christian will long for something more definitive and grow exasperated by its absence; an entire congregation will ponder whether it really belongs within this communion; bishops will gather to discuss an urgent matter and decide it deserves "further study." The courage required for doing this kind of faith did not, of course, first appear with Anglicans. It has marked the development of Christianity ever since the Apostle Paul wrote his letters to the earliest Christian communities, each of them struggling to make some sense of the intersection between new ideas, old traditions, and a diversity of cultural practices.

Embracing the struggle of doing Christian faith marks a good place to begin when searching for an Anglican identity. Anglican Christianity will not appear clearly or definitively in a creed, or a confession, or a liturgy, or any other historical document, nor can it be "explained" to anyone in a lecture or a sermon. It can only be lived, and over time it may not necessarily "make sense," but it will nurture the conditions for recognizing what the Apostle Paul called the "fruit of the Spirit" (Galatians 5:22). This is true of Christian faith generally, which is not something one simply knows or understands, like reading recipes in a cookbook or being told how gravity works. It's something one does and practices, like actually baking bread or climbing gracefully up a staircase. Ultimately, the point is not that you "made sense" of the recipe or that you "understood" gravity. You made bread and you didn't fall.

So also with this book, which is neither a recipe for becoming an Anglican nor an explanation of what "Anglicanism" means. It is, rather, an invitation to "do" Christian faith in a particularly Anglican way. Just as Anglican thinkers have done in the past, this invitation turns to the breadth of historical Christian traditions, digging and sifting through them for insights. A nineteenth-century Anglican theologian, F. D. Maurice, called this approach "grubbing." For me, Maurice conjures the image of rifling through the stacks of papers and scribbled notes on my desk searching for a half-remembered quote. It takes some work and I often wind up tossing much aside, but it's worth it to find that buried gem.

An Anglican approach to theology also stresses the public expression of Christian faith in the form of common prayer. This commitment to the primacy of prayer shared in common emerged early on in the Church of England at the hands of Thomas Cranmer, who was the primary architect of the Book of Common Prayer. The Prayer Book was not merely a practical tool for ensuring political stability in England (though it was surely that much). It also confirmed a more ancient insight about where the "data" for theology comes from—the worshipping life of a faith community. For Anglicans, any theological insight must stand the test of a community gathered for prayer and worship. By the same token, our liturgical texts themselves must stand the test of the insights we glean from praying together. The many revisions of the Prayer Book bear witness to this ongoing, mutual exchange between theological traditions and contemporary experience in Anglican Christianity.[2]

To do Anglican theology in this way means treating diversity as a blessing rather than as a curse, recognizing that truth never emerges all at once or from a single source but only from multiple perspectives in a concert of voices. William Temple, the Archbishop of Canterbury during World War II, put this insight into practice with his pioneering work in ecumenical dialogue. But the diversity in question here doesn't refer only to the variety we find in Christian denominations or in the long history of Christian traditions, but also to the insights we can discern apart from strictly "religious" sources, including the arts and culture, our social and political life, and what we continue to learn from the physical sciences about how the universe of God's creation works and holds together.

An Anglican invitation to do Christian faith invites reflection on all these sources and texts, on creeds and liturgies, on key figures from the past and the lessons learned from their struggles. It also turns, and just as much, to the hard work of conversation, the building and sustaining of a diverse community and living on the creative edges of ambiguity. Responding to such an invitation requires the courage to start dancing even if the music is unfamiliar and the steps feel a bit strange. It requires, in other words, the willingness to practice Christian faith—not with the certainty of "being right," but with the hope of joining the dance.

THE PRACTICE OF HOPE

In most academic disciplines, like most of life's projects, theories seem to work well on paper but rarely retain their clarity in practice. Planning a garden on paper is one thing; ensuring the plants will grow in exactly the way you intend is quite another. Learning the steps for a tango is relatively easy; dancing with a partner is hard. All of our projects and hobbies and fields of study present the vexing choice between the tidy lines of well-crafted design and the rough edges of the final product. When it comes to religious faith, Anglican Christians generally refuse to choose between either theory or practice, resisting the temptation to draw a distinct line between the two. This refusal springs from a deep conviction that what we believe as Christians ought necessarily to relate to how we live; we seek to match theories with real life. Indeed, "real life" in Anglican contexts involves a lot of thinking about what we're doing and not just doing it. Putting that conviction into practice continually raises vexing questions for which simple answers rarely suffice, especially in the midst of richly diverse cultural traditions and competing social priorities. In more traditional language, Christian theology and Christian ethics belong inseparably together, and while most Christians quickly acknowledge this link in theory, living it takes hard work.

A variety of factors, whether cultural, political, or academic, have made it even more difficult to discern the link between what Christians believe and how Christians live in the complexities of a twenty-first-century world. Most Christians would probably acknowledge the importance of various doctrines for their faith, like the idea of atonement or belief in God as Trinity. At the same time, many of them probably wonder how these doctrinal features of Christian faith relate to the practical realities of real life, to the questions raised by politics and social policy, like the deeply entrenched mechanisms of racism or the systemic perpetuation of poverty. Anglican theologians have insisted on connecting what appear to be purely "theoretical" concerns (like the Trinity) and the strictly "practical" ones (like racism). These aspects of Christian faith belong together, like the threads in a seamless garment. In Anglican circles, putting these links into practice is often referred to as "spirituality."

For Anglicans, spirituality means more than adopting a program of self-improvement, especially if such a program focuses on private, individualistic practices detached from "organized religion." American culture today abounds with this kind of self-help, programmatic approach as spirituality increasingly refers to doing something without thinking about it too much. Many of my religiously unaffiliated friends are eager to adopt a "spiritual practice" without all the baggage that comes with a "belief system."

When talking about spirituality, Anglicans mean something more deeply textured than an individual practice. It also turns out to be quite messy. Anglican Christians insist on forging the link between beliefs and actions, even when that intersection creates rough edges and a host of loose ends in our common life, as it inevitably does. Those untidy edges can create some discomfort and even profound anxiety in our interactions with each other. But they can also create an opportunity to learn about vulnerability and trust and to discover our lives changed in the crucible of shared love. This does not mean individual spiritual practices are irrelevant or unimportant in Anglican Christianity. It does mean that individual practices are rooted in a communal process. Mark McIntosh, an Episcopal priest and theologian, turns to early church sources to make a similar point about spirituality. In early Christianity, he writes, "individuals are not so much seeking to discover their own feelings as to live into the knowledge and love of God through the hard work of being members one with another of the Body of Christ." In this way, spirituality is "inherently mutual, communal and practical," oriented toward a new pattern of social and personal identity called church.[3]

Christian faith is inherently a social process in which insights for believing and living emerge from communal reflection and from which we learn to trust that the "doing" of our faith will yield more clarity over time. Engaging in this kind of social process, even when we are not entirely sure where that process will lead, marks a key feature of Anglican Christianity. The courage to forge ahead without a clearly defined blueprint is what I mean by "the practice of hope" in Anglican Christianity, and it gives shape to this book for two reasons.

First, if Christian faith describes a practice, just as much as it refers to what one believes, the practice in question is one of hope. Christian theology, to be Christian at all, must be hopeful, that is, full of hope. In a world so pervasively marked by violence and death, and with so many reasons to fall into despair, the good news of Christianity must offer reasons for hope. Christian hope, however, does not succumb to wishful thinking or to a nostalgic or idle wistfulness. It is not content merely to dream or envision a new world. Christian hope is restless and active, eager to put its energies into practice. And Christian hope receives its energy from a broad vision even if it doesn't operate from a detailed blueprint to achieve it: the kind of world where everyone can dance freely with the God of abundant life.

Second, Anglican Christianity describes a remarkably broad approach to Christian faith in which not just one but a variety of theologies can thrive and interact with each other. This diversity doesn't always rest easily or comfortably among us, and it does run the risk of appearing like a justification for fuzzy or muddled thinking. But the lack of just one "Anglican theology" does not render Anglican Christianity incoherent by definition. After all, the Christian scriptures retain their coherence even though they include four distinct gospels and varying theological approaches in the epistles. Generally speaking, Anglicans resist the temptation to force multiple biblical perspectives into a single method or system. Recognizing this range of perspectives in the Bible itself can soothe some of the anxiety our own diversity generates. Seeking insights from multiple sources and allowing space for a range of approaches endows Anglican Christianity with a fluid rather than a static or rigid coherence, which reflects the way in which historical Christian traditions developed over time. While this approach may contain considerable loose ends and frayed edges, it also invites us to dance with God in particularly vibrant ways.

Dancing, of course, takes on different forms and requires a variety of skills. There are many types of dancing; they vary depending on the musical genre, the underlying rhythm, and one's mood. Some of these types involve extensive training and learning elaborate steps, the rules of the choreography. Other types encourage more free-form engagements with the music, one's partners, and the social setting. There are significant differences, in other words, between square dancing and disco, but both of them are considered forms of dancing. The different types of dancing and the variety of skills required for each offer a way to think about Christian faith and theology. They can shape the way we speak about encounters with Divine Reality, open new entry points into theological traditions, and inspire creative ways to practice hope in each new situation and context in which we live out our faith.

In my experience, theological reflection can launch us on something like an adventure in which we discover new insights, explore strange worlds, and entertain previously unimagined possibilities for human thriving. Something similar happens on a dance floor. I've been to discos, sock hops, tango competitions, country-and-western line dances, and formal balls replete with elegant waltzes, and I have tried to dance in each of those ways at least once. Each time, I learn something new about myself, my body, my relationships, and how I interact with the world around me. On occasion, I also learn something about joy and love and intimacy. In this sense, among others, Christian theology and dancing belong together, and each of the following chapters will consider the implications of that claim for the link between Christian believing and Christian living.

Traditionally, books on Christian theology, especially "systematic theology," follow a recognizable pattern. They begin with a description of theological method, of how the work of theology proceeds with reference to sources, procedures, and goals. The method is then applied to the traditional doctrinal points of contact in Christian theology: who God is, how we know anything at all about God, what it means to be human and therefore sinful, why salvation is necessary and how it is accomplished, and by what means we live out this redeeming work in practice. As the theologian articulates each of these doctrinal areas of concern with reference to the methodological foundation, the doctrines begin to overlap and interlock with each other in systematic fashion.

I admire that traditional pattern for theology and will draw on its insights for this book, but not with the goal of creating a system. Anglican theologies don't easily lend themselves to intricate systems of thought. That's one of the strengths of Anglican styles of Christian faith—they create a bit more room on the edges of traditional theology for creativity and even playfulness. At the same time, this is not a book about starting from scratch or reinventing the wheel. It is, rather, an invitation to pause and notice what may have been left behind or forgotten in theological traditions, either through benign neglect or because of the inevitable bureaucratic staleness that comes with any human institution, including the church.

Cultural sensibilities and expectations can also create problems for Christian faith and theology. For many in modern Western societies, Hollywood films and television shows shape their understanding of the word "God" just as much as biblical texts and theological traditions. What people today mean by the word "God" is probably a complex mix of both religious teaching and popular cultural assumptions. In this book, I use the term "Divine Reality" as a synonym for "God," which I hope will encourage people to think outside the restrictive boxes in which Christian faith is so often contained. Some Christians likewise experiment with traditionally feminine imagery for the divine. By using "mother" rather than or in addition to "father" when speaking of Divine Reality, they try to break free from some of the gender-based patterns of abuse in Western culture to which masculine language in theology has contributed. I believe the image of dancing helps in the same way, an idea I invite you to test with me in the following chapters. Conducting this kind of test means sorting through the history of Christian traditions for insights into what it means to encounter Divine Reality and how those encounters inspire and urge us to live. Locating Christian faith at the inter-section of historical traditions and contemporary experience is one of the key strengths in Anglican Christianity. Putting that strength into practice requires the hard work of conversation to which I hope this book will make a contribution.

The first chapter considers questions of theological method. In the world of dancing, this means paying attention to the tools for learning a particular kind of choreography. In my experience with country-and-western dance lessons, I came to see how the rules of a given choreography exist for the sake of the dance itself, not the other way around. If fudging the traditional rules helps one dance, so much the better. The same insight applies to the way Anglican Christians have approached questions of theological method, or how to learn the dance steps inspired by encounters with God.

Choreography alone is obviously not sufficient for dancing; we need a place to practice the steps. Some types of dancing require a clearly defined space with all the standard elements neatly arranged, such as an uncluttered dance floor and a suitable bandstand. Sometimes the mood strikes rather suddenly and we push back the living room furniture, flip on the stereo, and invite our dinner guests to dance. In either case, dancing requires the foun-dation of a dance floor and the courage to step foot on it. The dance floor and the courage it inspires is what Anglican traditions mean by faith, which comes with no guarantee of doubt-free certainty (Chapter 2).

After considering the tools for learning how to dance and securing the dance floor itself, the next thing we need for dancing is some music. Nearly any kind of music will do, from the vibrant rhythms of a live band to the scratchy sounds of an old tape recording, or simply humming a tune and feeling the beat in our muscles while hiking in the mountains or strolling along a beach. Encounters with Divine Reality create their own kind of music, which often resists precise description. Sometimes we hear this music as clearly as a trumpet blast. At other times, it hovers gently in the back-ground, like a whisper. Mostly, we must train our ears to hear it. Discerning the strains of that divine music everywhere and all around us is what Christians mean by the love of the Holy Trinity, swelling up and spilling over into an invitation to dance. While anyone can hear this music at any time, Anglicans believe we hear it best in the company of others, where we can learn to recognize and practice the Trinitarian rhythms of conversation and conversion (Chapter 3).

As anyone who has ever danced knows, this process of learning the steps, clearing a space, and hearing the music does not always proceed along such carefully planned trajectories. Dancing, just like human life itself, doesn't always follow prescribed steps or established patterns. Nearly every form of choreography emerges from particular cultural traditions, some of which feel familiar and comfortable while others seem strange and slightly exotic. Christian faith pushes us beyond our usual comfort zones to discern what a genuinely human dance with God looks like. The doctrine of the Incarnation has been one of the key ways Christian traditions have tried to understand how the fullness of human life, with all its particular foibles and follies, all its toil and laughter, is brought explicitly into the orbit of Divine Reality. Anglicans have turned frequently to this doctrine, almost like a mantra. In Chapter 4 I'll consider the dance steps Jesus invites us to learn for the sake of human thriving.

Learning how to dance and how to dance well, especially with a partner, involves both discipline and a fairly rigorous regimen of practice. It requires the intentional adoption of particular habits, which Christian traditions have referred to as "spirituality." Anglican Christians generally link spiritual practice to the regular rhythms of institutional church life while still recognizing the limits of religious institutions in our dance with God. Embracing rather than lamenting those limits creates some breathing space in Anglican traditions for encountering the seductive and restless energy of the dance itself. Chapter 5 explores how Christian traditions have identified this energy as the Holy Spirit and how this energy inspires Anglican approaches to spirituality.

Christian faith and theology, just like dancing, enjoy both individual and social expressions. I might, for example, do a little jig in the privacy of my own home upon receiving some particularly happy news. At other times, that same news urges me to dance with other people, like joining a conga line during a wedding reception. The good news of Christian faith, which we hear distinctly as individuals, inevitably inspires a communal dance. Indeed, Christian hope is primarily a social hope; dancing with God is by definition a corporate activity. In Christian traditions, this hope has been expressed by interacting with and participating in the institution called church, which raises a host of questions about the complex relationship between religion and culture and between institutional texts and communal practices. Anglican Christians insist on the importance of institutional or "organized" forms of religion while still maintaining a critical distance from the abuses of institutional power and authority. This precarious posture toward church springs from the hope of communion, from the hope of enacting a genuinely communal dance with God. The institutional church can point to this hope, but only as a sign of that communion which has yet to be realized (Chapter 6).

Throughout these chapters I will keep returning to a key feature of Anglican traditions: What Christians believe (theology) is inseparable from how we believe it (ethics). Most Christian communities recognize the importance of ethics, but Anglicans don't usually treat ethics as "merely" the practical application of theological ideas. For some Christians, theology remains fixed and unchangeable, while the application of theology in our conduct of life varies depending on the circumstances. Anglicans understand the relationship between theology and ethics more dynamically, as something like a two-way street. What we learn in the practice of our Christian faith shapes the content of that faith, and vice versa. Anglicans continually reach toward that dynamic exchange between theology and ethics, even when we have trouble knowing how to put it into practice. Studying and reflecting on the links between believing and doing will help us dance better as Anglicans, but it won't lead to "getting things right." It will, rather, help us notice and celebrate how Christian theology generates a remarkably wide array of possibilities for putting Christian hope into practice.

The practice of hope as it unfolds in these chapters doesn't lead to a conclusion in the traditional sense. Instead, the final chapter will consider some of the ways in which traditional religious approaches no longer inspire joining the dance as they once did. As contemporary Western societies exhibit an increasing hunger for a more explicitly spiritual engagement with life, traditional religion too often falls short of addressing that hunger. Moreover, the many ways in which Christians have stumbled on the dance floor can raise significant doubts about embracing institutional church life. These are some of the factors contributing to today's "postmodern" condition and to the appearance of what I like to call "hopeful wallflowers" at the Christian dance, the ones who are intrigued by the potential in Christian faith but wary about joining the dance uncritically. Taking that wariness seriously offers prospects for a twenty-first-century dance and for discerning how Anglican Christians can dance to postmodern music.

If there is a conclusion to draw from this kind of work, it surely comes down to this: God continues to extend the invitation to dance to all of us. Once we catch even a glimpse of it, or hear even a few notes of that divine music, it changes our lives and the lives of those around us. As it does, we will want to study how others have danced in the past. We will want to analyze the steps, consider the choreography, and train our ears to hear the music as clearly as we can. We will want to designate specific spaces for the dance and create the best conditions possible for practicing the steps. All of these are important impulses and tasks, and each of them plays a role in the various theological disciplines Christians have developed over the centuries. They are important, but they are not the dance itself.

Christian theology remains Christian insofar as it helps us think about our life with God in the same way we think about a wedding: God desires us and has fallen in love with us. This startling truth about reality invites us to dance and it is the job of the Christian theologian to help us dance better. To that end, we don't need to ask the clergy among us to serve as disc jockeys for wedding receptions; they have plenty to do already. It will be enough when we are no longer surprised to see them on the dance floor.

1

WALTZING THE TWO-STEP
~ A Hopeful Theological Method ~

Learning how to dance and learning how to "do" Christian faith have a
great deal in common. The theological potential in this connection occurred
to me some years ago, when I was introduced to country-and-western dancing. Before then, I had not paid much attention to country music, but the
dancing looked like a lot of fun. With some encouragement from friends, I
decided to take lessons.

The instructor tried to reassure us by saying how simple this kind of
dancing is to learn. We began with the two-step. "All you need to know," the
instructor said, "is two sets of steps. The first is slow, the second quick:
slow . . . slow, quick-quick, slow . . . slow, quick-quick." After a brief demon-
stration (which really did make it look easy), he reminded us that two-
stepping is only one kind of country-and-western dance. So we also learned
steps for the traditional waltz, which requires a different kind of count: one,
two, three and one, two, three, and so on. The underlying rhythm of a given
piece of music determines which of these steps to follow.

I had much more trouble with the two-step than I did with the waltz.
The concept of two-stepping seemed easy; actually performing the steps was
hard. After several instructional sessions over a number of weeks, I still wasn't
comfortable with matching the two-step count to the rhythm of the music.

I remained hopeful and tried my best, but I grew increasingly frustrated with my stumbling feet. I started to avoid two-stepping music and waited for waltzes.

Then one day, after complaining about my apparent lack of two-stepping ability, a friend made a deceptively simple suggestion. "Just use the waltz count for the two-step," he said. This confused me at first—how can you count to three for a two-step? Then I tried it, with the slight modification he recommended. Rather than "one, two, three and," I tried "one, two, and three and, one, two, and three and." It worked. Adding the extra "and" in the count made my feet move a bit more quickly on the "ands" and a bit slower on the numbers, matching precisely the rhythm of the music for a two-step.

Not everyone has the same kind of trouble with the two-step as I did, and for those who do, two-stepping to a waltz count may not work as well as it did for me. But I gained two insights from that experience. First, the rules of dancing are meant to help you dance better, not the other way around. Dancing well serves the dance itself, not the rules. After all, the point is to learn how to dance, and if you can learn to dance by fudging the rules, so much the better. Second, by learning how to two-step by using a waltz count, the world of dancing opened up for me in a new way. Before long, I was whirling around the dance floor without bothering to count at all (or even look at my feet!). The rules slowly faded away and only the dancing remained.

I soon carried those insights off the dance floor and into my theological work. I realized that dancing with God, just like the two-step, requires some instruction. We need to learn the "dance steps" of the divine-human encounter. Yet these rules and procedures in theological traditions are tools to help us dance in encounters with Divine Reality, not the other way around. The point is the encounter itself, and if the given procedures at hand prove troubling or less than helpful, it's probably time to adjust the procedures.

Rule fudging certainly seems appropriate for something like dancing; it seems a bit less so for questions of theological method. Hardly anyone I know would insist on making the rules for two-stepping more important than actually doing the two-step. Yet in the history of Christian theological traditions, religious rules and procedures have sometimes eclipsed encounters with Divine Reality, which those procedures were designed to facilitate. Consider the place of honor given to the Bible in theological method. What do we do when a theological insight—uncovered in prayer, perhaps—casts some doubt on the usefulness of a particular biblical passage? Or consider a particularly well-loved and cherished liturgical tradition, a particular phrase learned in childhood, perhaps, or a stylized gesture. What do we do when that tradition creates friction in how our community feels moved to worship together? In situations such as these, some Christians continue to rely on the biblical text and the liturgical tradition at the expense of their own experience; others feel compelled to abandon those ancient touchstones altogether. As I discovered on that country-and-western dance floor, there is another option. We could choose to waltz the two-step.

Whenever Jesus addressed this kind of dilemma, he refused both the static preservation of tradition and its outright disposal. Consider his apparent violation of Sabbath observance, to which Jesus responded with a creative insight we would do well to take to heart. "The sabbath was made for humankind," he said, "not humankind for the sabbath" (Mark 2:27). Note that Jesus didn't disparage the Sabbath just by breaking some of its rules. Likewise, in my experience with country-and-western dancing, I did not abandon the two-step just because I learned how to do it better by using a waltz count. In fact, just the opposite is true in both cases: The two-step and the Sabbath are taken more seriously by adjusting the rules to achieve them.

Human beings are frequently tempted to follow the procedures of religious traditions whether or not those procedures actually facilitate encounters with Divine Reality. We might do this for reasons of comfort and safety or perhaps we're simply unaware of alternatives. This approach carries the risk of mistaking the procedures for the encounter itself, as if the point is to master the rules. Worrying only about the rules of religious traditions is not so different from learning the two-step count without ever stepping foot on the dance floor. The result is a static, rather wooden form of religious faith that severely limits our ability to recognize an encounter with Divine Reality when we stumble into it. And we will stumble, as the many stories from Christian traditions illustrate. Remember the conversion of the Apostle Paul, who didn't merely stumble but fell to the ground in an encounter with the risen Christ (Acts 9:4).

If we manage to avoid an obsession with rules and procedures, we might slip into the opposite dynamic and be tempted to forgo any instruction for the dance at all, preferring instead to make it up as we go along. Innovation certainly has its place, both on the dance floor and in the life of faith. At the same time, the excitement and energy such innovation generates can tempt us to ignore the methods and insights of previous generations. Americans seem particularly vulnerable to this latter temptation, which our history of courageous pioneering and creative invention clearly demonstrates. In fact, very little of American inventiveness would have been possible apart from the many generations of European inquiry, investigation, and experiment that preceded it. In theological terms, try reading the gospels without any reference to the history of Israel; those gospel stories would make very little sense.

Both of these temptations have always marked the Christian theological landscape, but they are particularly well ensconced today. Some Christians clearly fret over the prospect of abandoning historical traditions while others no longer find those traditions useful or insightful. Anglicans have come to realize that Christian theology evolves over time and is never quite finished, and that while inventiveness plays an important role, Christian faith is not a matter of creating the resources we need from scratch. Situating ourselves on that creative edge of faith is the work of theological method, or how we "do" theology. Like any discipline or skill, the method for engaging in the work of theology relies on a variety of tools. Broadly speaking, those tools include the Hebrew and Christian scriptures that make up the Bible, our creeds and liturgies, and our own experience and desires as we interact with those around us and the wider society in which we live.

Forging an adequate theological method from these basic tools has always involved considerable reflection and multiple modes of analysis in Christian history. The earliest Christians lived without any canon or officially recognized collection of Christian scripture. Christian communities scattered throughout the Roman Empire learned from their own insights, turned to the guidance of local leaders and occasionally to a circulating letter or treatise for discerning what it means to be a Christian and to live a Christian life. This approach to Christian faith and theology took a decisive turn in the fourth century, when the Roman Emperor Constantine made Christianity the official religion of the empire. Some of those circulating documents, including gospels and letters by the Apostle Paul, were collected and, after considerable debate, organized into the normative texts of Christian scripture. At the same time, particular church leaders, usually bishops, started to exercise new kinds of authority and to meet together to resolve questions about Christian belief and practice. The Council of Nicaea, for example, meeting in 325, drafted what became known as the Nicene Creed, a baseline for standard Christian belief, which most Anglican communities continue to recite every Sunday morning. In these first few centuries, in other words, the texts of scripture and church tradition developed into two distinct yet interrelated sources of insight for Christian faith. Add to this mix the cultural and political context of the Roman Empire, and a rather diverse set of tools starts to emerge for crafting a theological method.

Today every Christian denomination and community face new questions and not a few problems in discerning how to do its theological work. Historical research and developments in the social sciences continually shed new light on biblical texts. Appreciating the economic and political contexts in which church traditions evolve adds new layers of complexity to the creeds and liturgies inherited from the past. In a world of global communication, differences in language, custom, and culture become more apparent and highlight the inadequacy of just one perspective. How do all of these various sources, discoveries, insights, and approaches interact? Where can Christian communities turn for help in evaluating the many different strands of Christian belief and practice? What do we really hope to accomplish with the tools of theological method?

Remembering why we do the work of theology can sometimes prove as difficult as discerning a proper method for doing it. Sorting through the complex interactions between religion and culture, between historical traditions and contemporary insights, can quickly obscure the fact that theology begins with desire—with *God's* desire. God has fallen in love with us and invites us to dance. At its best, Christian theology ought to serve as an invitation into the mystery of that Divine Reality, into God's own longing to see each of us thrive with abundant life. In this sense, Christian churches and their theological method resemble a dance studio. As students arrive, eager to learn how to move their bodies gracefully and rhythmically, they discover a variety of tools at their disposal: a wooden bar to help them stretch their muscles; mirror-lined walls in which to evaluate how their bodies move; a stereo to play some music; and the experience of an instructor. A dance studio does not exist merely for the sake of preserving or displaying those tools; the dance studio puts those tools to use to help people dance.

Switch metaphors for a moment and consider the work of gardening and home improvement, tasks that require good tools. When we're organized and have the requisite space, we'll make sure to store what we need in a toolbox, which we might keep in a backyard shed. When we build the shed to hold the box that contains the tools, we are not therefore finished, as if the purpose of the tools is merely to possess them and find a safe place to store them. The purpose of tools, whether a hammer or a watering can, is to use them for something else, to assist us in our building and fixing, our nesting and playing, our growing and resting.

Like the dance studio and the backyard shed, Christian churches contain a variety of tools. Discerning how to put those tools to use is the work of theological method. This process includes interpreting biblical texts, engaging with creedal and liturgical traditions, and incorporating insights from contemporary experience. As dance instructors and homeowners know, however, the same tools can produce widely different results depending on how they are used and who uses them.

The same thing applies to Christianity. There is more than one way to use the tools of Christian theology, as the wide array of approaches to Christian faith in today's many denominations clearly demonstrates. Anglican Christians usually know that their own dance is similar to but also different from how other Christians are dancing. Discerning these differences and learning how to dance like an Anglican takes time and usually a good deal of patience. The tools for such learning are readily available, but figuring out how to use them can be perplexing.

LEARNING ANGLICAN DANCE STEPS

I like all sorts of dancing. Sometimes free-form improvisation satisfies my longing to dance and to use whatever skills I have for creativity and innovation. I also enjoy learning particular steps for a specific form because I constantly wish I were a better dancer. Sometimes these desires overlap, like they did when I learned to waltz the two-step: Innovation improved the rules. Both of these desires play an important role in theological method, and I suspect many Anglicans experience both of these impulses simultaneously in Anglican approaches to Christian faith. The desire to dance like an Anglican remains strong, but we're not always sure how to do it.

Inquirers' classes in the Episcopal Church try to address this desire by introducing the classic touchstones of Anglican theological method. Many Episcopalians know these touchstones well enough to admire them: the *via media*, or middle way between Protestantism and Catholicism; the "three-legged stool" of scripture, tradition, and reason; and the unifying symbol of the Book of Common Prayer. Taken together, these touchstones suggest a way to use the tools of Christian theology, a general method for interpreting biblical texts or appropriating doctrinal insights or shaping our worship. Over time, however, this method poses more questions than it can answer. How do we know when we have drifted into one of the extremes rather than navigating the "middle way"? Why has one of the "legs" of our stool become too short, making us list or wobble when we try to sit on it? Can the Prayer Book provide unity when it remains vulnerable to constant revision and our liturgical language seems so unstable? The Anglican dance studio provides plenty of tools, but it's not entirely clear how to use them for creating a graceful dance.

This kind of quandary didn't suddenly emerge in the sixteenth-century English Reformation. Christians have always worried about using theological tools properly and correctly. The Apostle Paul devoted significant portions of his letters to correcting the theological misconceptions of the Christian communities to which he wrote. The gradual emergence of orthodoxy and heresy as decisive theological categories marked the development of the ecumenical councils, like the Council of Nicaea. The Protestant Reformation, rather than prompting fundamental reform in the institutional church, generated the profound fragmentation of Christian identities with which we now live, where each denomination offers the promise of "doing" Christian faith better. Each of these historical moments shares the same theological tools, but the method for using them looks a bit different in each case.

Anglican anxiety over a proper theological method, while not new, exhibits a peculiar energy. Rather than worrying about being theologically correct, Anglican Christians often worry about worrying too much about such correctness. After all, Anglican Christianity carries with it the reputation of tolerance and diversity by offering a wide religious embrace (the *via media*), a well-balanced and sensible approach to theological insight (the three-legged stool), and a malleable yet unifying liturgical tradition (the Prayer Book). Anglicans who consider themselves "conservative" as well as those who consider themselves "liberal" can adopt this kind of method, and both groups insist they are doing so "correctly." Before long, Anglican Christians begin to wonder in what, exactly, an Anglican identity consists. What does it really mean to dance like an Anglican?

Anglicans have lived with this question and its attendant anxiety ever since King Henry VIII severed his ties with the Pope in the sixteenth century and declared himself the "Supreme Head of the Church in England." It was not at all clear what kind of church body this action created. It was not a Protestant church in the same way Martin Luther's reform movement was Protestant. (Henry was actually firmly opposed to the Lutheran "heresy.") But without its explicit ties to Rome, the Church in England could no longer be considered Catholic either.

Anglicans usually prefer to locate our origins a bit later, during the reign of Elizabeth I, when the Book of Common Prayer offered a way to unite English society divided by Catholic and Protestant sensibilities. This worked for a time, in what became known as the "Elizabethan Settlement," but it never really addressed whether the English church operated theologically (in terms of its method) or even spiritually (in how it worshipped) in any way that was distinct from its Roman counterpart or from its more firmly established Protestant cousins on the Continent. Richard Hooker, in trying to sort through these issues late in the sixteenth century, published what became one of the classic attempts to describe this peculiarly Anglican approach. In his multivolume work, *The Laws of Ecclesiastical Polity*, Hooker refuted arguments put forth by the Puritans, who were gaining in both influence and political power in England. By arguing for both the authority of the Bible and the authority of the church in England in configuring its own institutional life, Hooker tried to map out a new and rather paradoxical kind of religious space, one that is both Catholic and Protestant at the same time.

Today, as differences and disagreements become more apparent in the worldwide Anglican Communion, questions of Anglican identity have taken on added urgency. As always with Anglicans, contemporary challenges invite a reconsideration of theological method, of how we use the theological tools at our disposal. The benefits of reflecting on such questions extend well beyond finding a way to sort through the particular machinations of Anglican Church politics. These methodological issues cut to the heart of Christian faith generally and not only its Anglican expressions. Learning to dance like an Anglican can offer some important insights into what it means to be a Christian at all.

Theological work of the sort I'm describing here resembles my experience of trying to learn the two-step. Changing my perspective on that dance floor by using the waltz count for a two-step came rather quickly, even though it seemed odd at first. In Christian theology, it will take a bit more courage to make a similar shift. As I discovered with the two-step, the dance itself must be the priority, which is precisely what theological method is supposed to help us accomplish—to dance better with God. Making the dance our priority may mean calling into question some of its traditional procedures, even the ones that have made the most sense in the past if they aren't working as well as they used to. The challenges Anglicans face today may mean the time has come to waltz the two-step in Christian theology. The Anglican three-legged stool of scripture, tradition, and reason offers a good place to begin.

When faced with nearly any theological or moral dilemma (though most often the latter), Anglicans resort almost immediately and in some fashion to the three legs of that stool. We turn first to scripture and try to discern whether any of the biblical authors address the issue at hand. We turn next to the traditions of the church, whether in the form of ecumenical councils or recognized theological authorities from the past, and try to search out any further insight for the question. Finally, we examine the topic through the lens of our own God-given reason, now rightly expanded to include "experience," which amplifies what we mean by reason by including affectivity, intuition, social context, and so on. The goal throughout this procedure is to give each of these legs its due and to construct a balanced approach in which none of the three legs trumps the other two.

While this method works beautifully on paper, it rarely lives up to its promise in practice. As anyone who has tried to apply it knows, one of the "legs" inevitably wins, throwing the stool off balance. Yet this is not a case of merely trying harder to make it work. Let's say, for example, in searching the traditions we find the work of Augustine, a fourth-century theological pioneer, who seems to speak directly to the particular question at hand. As we dutifully select an appropriate text, we realize that Augustine can hardly write more than a sentence of his own without quoting scripture. So which of the three legs are we turning to here, tradition or scripture? Upon further examination, we realize that the process of selecting Augustine in the first place depends on using our reason and experience to make that choice, rather than, say, a text from Tertullian or Aquinas. Likewise, Augustine himself turned to his own experience and social context when deciding which part of the scripture to quote. If we decide to go back to square one and sift through the scriptures themselves, the same complexities quickly mar the tidy edges of this method. The biblical writers also drew on their own religious traditions based on their own experiences and social contexts. And, of course, the process that led us to a particular passage among those writers depends in large measure on our own experiences and our reading of the traditions, which we invariably bring to our reading of biblical texts. Who can say which of the "legs" of our stool we are talking about at any given moment?

Perhaps the problem rests with the image itself and how quickly the metaphor breaks down. The legs of a stool and the stool itself are all things, objects we can touch, hammer together, trip over, and adorn with a cushion. Scripture, tradition, and reason are decidedly not things in the same way. Imagine actually trying to make a real stool out of those "things." Metaphors, of course, aren't supposed to be taken literally; that's why the stool is not really a stool, but a metaphor. But even metaphorically there are problems. Consider again the hypothetical example of finding an insight from Augustine's writings. Part of the reason the metaphorical stool fails is precisely because the legs of a real stool don't interact with each other in the same way scripture, Augustine's writings, and our experience interact. The legs of a stool are static, rigidly separated, and never touch each other. That's why stools support people who sit on them. The same is rarely if ever true for the "legs" of scripture, tradition, and reason. They constantly blend together, frustrating nearly every attempt to separate them into individual, clearly defined "legs."

What Anglicans have wanted to say by using the image of the three-legged stool is actually confounded by the image itself. Those who employ it seem to want to say something like this: We are suspicious of appealing to biblical texts apart from the insights gleaned from historical-critical method, literary criticism, or human reason. At the same time, we are suspicious of appealing to rational principles if these are made at the expense of aesthetic or affective principles. Yet we are also suspicious of appealing to human experience unless it is informed by biblical insights, resources in the human sciences, and theological traditions. We are suspicious of all these things, not because we want clearly to identify our sources, but precisely because we know these sources interact with each other in complex ways. Rather than a stool, theological method is more like a dance. In a dance, one's legs actually move.[1]

These are dance studio reflections, the kind of work dancers do before stepping foot on the dance floor. It's also the kind of work they return to after dancing for a while and they discover they want to dance better. The priority in both cases is the dance itself. Staying focused on the dance puts theological work in proper perspective and orients our reflections in a particular way, toward a hopeful theological method. In a world marked so deeply by the temptation to despair—by job loss, divorce, illness, grinding and unrelenting poverty, deeply entrenched racial and economic oppression, or the perpetual turn to violence to solve disputes—in all of these, human beings search for hope and seek ways to be hopeful. We want, in other words, to respond to God's invitation to dance. In this sense, learning to dance like an Anglican can inspire hope and, in turn, offer some idea of what it looks like to put hope into practice.

ACCOUNTING FOR HOPE

Anglican Christians understand the dynamic interaction of scripture, tradition, and our experience not as the dance itself, but as a way to learn the choreography. We can give ourselves permission to worry about these tools of our method and how to use them if we remember that such worrying is for the sake of the dance and not merely for the method. Not just the theology created from the method, but also the method itself can be hopeful when we no longer feel compelled to treat Christianity like a rare book in need of preservation. Theological method has more in common with my country-and-western dancing friend, who suggested I try the waltz count for a two-step, or with a dance instructor who doesn't mind if we fudge the rules as long as we get out on the dance floor.

These perpetually unfinished and malleable qualities of Christian theology reflect the dynamic qualities of human encounters with Divine Reality. In the Gospels, Jesus insisted that these encounters are not confined within the rules of a given religious tradition. Indeed, the human tendency to worry over proper rules and procedures can sometimes obscure the encounter itself. This does not make rules, procedures, and methods inherently distracting as long as their purpose is kept in view. As biblical writers frequently demonstrate, even the most meticulously designed method can't account for the surprising insights discovered in encounters with Divine Reality. Some of the most cherished stories from Israel's history sounded unsettling when Jesus told them with a new perspective. Familiar religious customs concerning food and dietary practices suddenly seemed out of place among the newly converted Gentiles with whom the Apostle Paul worked. Cultural assumptions about marriage and family were scrutinized and reevaluated in the experiences of creating Christian community. In all these ways and more, Christian theology struggles to keep up with the encounters and experiences that inspired it, like trying to transcribe on paper the fluid lines and multiple steps of a tango. Rather than cause for dismay, the dynamic character of Christian theology makes Christian faith a matter of genuinely good news. As Divine Reality dances before our eyes, it tantalizes us with the possibility that we too can join the dance, even when we are still uncertain about the steps. This, in more traditional language, is called hope.

"Always be ready," says the biblical writer, "to make your defense to anyone who demands from you an accounting for of the hope that is in you" (1 Peter 3:15). This short, rather unassuming biblical exhortation neatly summarizes the purpose in Christian theological work, both in terms of method ("being ready") and theology ("giving an account"). This biblical writer assumes, of course, that his readers are hopeful to begin with, which raises questions about the content of Christian hope. The word "hope" itself, a word that appears in all sorts of contexts and can refer to a wide range of aspirations, deserves scrutiny.

Human beings rarely, if ever, experience hope generally; it is almost always attached to specifics. We might hope for reconciliation in a fractured relationship. We might hope to find a loving partner with whom to share our lives. We might hope our children will grow up in a less violent, more economically stable world. We might hope for more simple things as well—that the tulip bulbs planted in winter will grow and bloom in the spring, or that the pear tree in the backyard will bear fruit after its severe pruning. Hope takes a variety of forms, yet always with reference to specifics. Christian theology, on the other hand, continually inspires new ways to speak about the specific content of Christian hope, which is sometimes quite concrete and, at other times, just beyond our grasp.

In his letter to the Romans, Paul leaves no room for doubt about the importance of hope, yet seems ultimately unwilling to define it with precision. "Now hope that is seen is not hope," Paul writes. "For who hopes for what is seen?" (Romans 8:24). Whatever we already know or possess, in other words, is not something for which we still hope. In this sense, Christian hope differs significantly from optimism. An optimistic view of the world sees little that is fundamentally wrong with how things presently stand. While some minor adjustments are probably required, the world is basically on track the way it is. Hope, on the other hand, is perpetually restless as it reaches toward the unseen. Hope brings one's own life, or the configurations of culture and society, or the inner workings of an institution, under constant scrutiny. Hope is born from dissatisfaction with how things stand yet refuses to despair, believing that change, growth, and development are always possible, even if the ultimate goal of such growth eludes our grasp.

Being prepared to give an account of Christian hope—not just once but "always," as the biblical writer put it—infuses the life of faith with the perpetually restless and dynamic qualities of hope itself. Historical interpretations of scripture may not suffice for the present. Perhaps the language inherited from creedal statements no longer articulates adequately what Christians have come to believe today. Multicultural, twenty-first-century realities might not resonate with fourth-century Latin liturgical forms. At the same time, Christian hope still draws on the usefulness of scripture, tradition, and our God-given reason, and especially from the way we put these tools to use. For the sake of that hope, Anglicans don't really want a stool to sit on; we want legs to dance with.

Anglican theologies have tried to embrace both the instability and the potential in this dynamic approach to theological method, which offers a rich opportunity today and not only for discerning what it means to be an Anglican Christian. This kind of work can also be a gift to offer to other traditions confronting similar challenges. Ultimately, the three-legged stool, the *via media*, and Prayer Book traditions deserve dynamic reconfigurations for the sake of the good news they try to articulate and to offer the help we need to dance with God and with each other.

Reflecting on the traditional Anglican approach to theological method, the practice of hope appears in at least the following four ways. Each of these gives shape to doing Christian faith in a particularly Anglican way, and I offer them as a way to waltz our Anglican two-step. I trust this will help all of us dance better, not for the sake of "getting it right," but as a way of putting Christian hope into practice.

The Commitment to Conversation

Anglican Christians have never been comfortable with faith by decree, whether from a monarch or a bishop. Anglican history certain exhibits the attempt on occasion, whether by English kings and queens or by particularly strong-willed diocesan prelates. But the attempt always fails. Possibly because of peculiar historical circumstances, creative personalities, divine inspiration, or a combination of all three, Anglican Christians have learned that neither morality nor theological insight can be legislated or coerced. Truth never emerges all at once but only gradually, over time, and by drawing on the perspectives and experiences of a wide range of traditions and groups.

Anglicans have, in other words, learned to rely on conversation for hammering out what it means to be a Christian. This doesn't make the life of faith any easier; just the opposite is the case. In some respects, it would be far easier to have theology handed down in a fixed text from the hands of an established authority. This rarely works with the more mundane aspects of human life and even less so in encounters with Divine Reality.[2]

A genuine conversation is never etched in stone. It relies on an open exchange of ideas, opinions, arguments, experiences, feelings, guesses, objections, and proposals, and all for the sake of teasing out truth as best as we can perceive it. A genuine conversation, furthermore, always carries the potential for conversion. (Both of these words, in fact, come from the same linguistic root.) Speaking the truth about our lives to each other invariably changes us, and not just once but continually. The commitment to ongoing, genuine conversation is one way to practice the hope of changed lives, for in such hope we can find resources for building communities of conversion in which conversation transpires more freely.

The Acknowledgment of Fallibility

Genuine conversation never fully comes to an end, just as the work of Christian conversion never reaches a final culmination. This means that each of us, right now, is mistaken about something and has more to learn. Anglican Christians have been willing, often remarkably so, to understand that faithfulness is not synonymous with flawlessness. Our faithfulness as Christians does not depend on living a mistake-free life. Indeed, a deeper kind of faithfulness emerges when we realize we have been terribly mistaken about this or that aspect of our lives or of the world around us. In this sense, faith develops over time and is subject to the same kind of hairpin turns and surprising course corrections experienced in nearly every other aspect of human living.

Human beings understandably wish to avoid the possibility of looking foolish, of holding on to and acting from a conviction that turns out to be misinformed. But nothing can prevent us from taking action more quickly than the anxiety over the possibility of being wrong. This is particularly true for religious convictions, in which human beings have invested a great deal for articulating the meaning of life itself.

Some religious traditions try to alleviate the anxiety created by human fallibility by insisting their convictions derive directly from divine revelation, which by definition cannot be mistaken. Anglicans likewise rely on revelation for guidance but understand that such revelation comes to us only through the complex filters of fallible human perception and layers of shifting cultural contexts. For this reason, communities of faith are communities of interpretation, locations of ongoing discernment marked by the struggle that comes from articulating the mysterious qualities and energies of encounters with Divine Reality. The practice of hope emerges whenever we acknowledge our human fallibility, an acknowledgment that creates the conditions for sustaining genuine conversation over the long haul.

The Reliance on Common Prayer

The dynamics of theological conversation transpire in a variety of locations, including such obvious places as diocesan conventions or vestry meetings or other venues where institutional matters are regularly evaluated and considered. For Anglicans, however, theological conversation happens best in our liturgical life. The reputation Anglicans have for perpetually fussing with liturgical forms creates the impression that we care mostly about putting on a good show. Actually, I see nothing wrong with that. As anyone involved in theater or in a dance company knows, wanting to put on a good show or caring about the quality of a given performance comes from realizing what happens when we do. In a good show, both performers and audience members are swept away and caught up in something larger than they are. In the same way, there is more going on in Prayer Book battles than merely fretting over furniture and costumes.

Liturgy offers tools and space for creating genuine conversations. We converse with scripture, with the traditions, and with the experiences of those gathered with us. We fuss over those tools and that space precisely because we know what is at stake in the kind of conversation that ought to happen on such occasions. Our liturgical life is nothing less than the opportunity to encounter Divine Reality, prompt deeper conversion, and nurture our relationships as God's people.

This doesn't mean, however, that prayer in common is uniform prayer. If we fuss with our liturgical texts from the desire to get it right or to ensure that everyone prays in exactly the same way, we have missed the point of true conversation and conversion. We also miss the same point when we try to create liturgies from scratch, as if the long and varied history of Christian prayer, stretching over many centuries, has no relevance for our contemporary communities. Living in that intersection of historical traditions and contemporary experience will not generate perfect or unchangeable liturgies. It will, however, make for lively conversation, the possibility of conversion, and the conditions for genuinely hopeful insights. Relying on Prayer Book traditions facilitates this kind of creative work, not by restricting how we ought to pray, but by providing a suitable dance floor on which to learn and experiment with the choreography that faith inspires.

Rather than trying to get it right, our liturgical fussing comes from a more deeply held conviction: Theological insight emerges best not from isolated reflection, but from those moments when people of faith pray together. By offering common prayer—the prayer created together as the community of God's people—we practice the hope of encountering Divine Reality in ways we never could on our own, as individuals.

The Embrace of Liminality

Genuine conversation among fallible human beings, prayerfully offered around a eucharistic table of shared bread and wine, points beyond itself to a reality we have yet to know and embrace in its fullness. It pushes us toward that which is still unseen and therefore toward hope. Meanwhile, we catch only a glimpse and receive only a taste of what it means to live the life God intends for us. Preserving a snapshot of that life will not suffice. Freeze-framing a movie provides only an inkling of the story still to unfold. We always have more to learn about how to dance.

The concept of liminality can help us here. It derives from the word "limen," for "threshold," like what we find in the doorways of our houses and other buildings. Anthropologists have used this word as a way to describe rites of passage, that phase of transition when a person, usually a teenager, has not yet passed over into adulthood but is no longer exactly a child, either. This person stands at a threshold, experiencing a liminal existence of not quite leaving one phase of life and not quite being fully engaged in the next.

The sixteenth-century emergence of the Church of England looked quite liminal. It never quite left its Catholic roots behind, nor fully stepped across the threshold into the Protestant Reformation. It looks wishy-washy and probably a bit gangly, like most teenagers do on the edge of adulthood.

These historical peculiarities inherent in any discussion of Anglican identity point more broadly to the liminal quality of Christianity itself. Who we are as Christian people is never finally fixed, static, and done. We sit perpetually on the threshold of self-definition, holding on to what we have learned in the past but knowing that the future will look and feel different. We hold on to the lessons of childhood as indispensable resources, yet we cannot now imagine how we will draw on them for the adventure that lies ahead.

Embracing our liminality puts hope into practice whenever we treat diversity as a gift rather than as a threat. Hope urges us to welcome fresh perspectives from unlikely sources, knowing that the work of becoming the people God intends is not yet finished. Hope persuades us that our own resources for that work will not suffice. It pushes us into the unknown to seek the gifts only a diverse community can offer.

By the same token, embracing our liminality doesn't mean attaching ourselves indiscriminately to anything that happens to be new or different. That's why the lessons learned from the past remain important and vital for moving into the future. But the past is not something merely to preserve, either. Hope inevitably makes us restless, urging us to apply those lessons in new ways. Embracing liminality can relieve the anxiety such restlessness usually creates. As many of the biblical writers tried to show, a liminal existence promises a new reality even if we cannot yet see it clearly. The Johannine writer, for example, reflects Paul's insight about an unseen hope: "Beloved, we are God's children now; what we will be has not yet been revealed" (1 John 3:2).

These four ways of practicing Christian hope may surprise newcomers to religious faith and even some lifelong Christians. Constructing an approach for theological reflection from the art of *conversation*, the acknowledgment of *fallibility*, the shifting currents of *common prayer*, and the uncertainty of a *liminal existence* seems far removed from the precision usually associated with methodological procedures. Assumptions about religion and religious authority in popular culture contribute to the frequently high-charged issues involved in theological method.

Religion has the reputation, often well deserved, of consisting in dogmatic doctrine, ethical rule keeping, and carefully constructed ritual. Those traditional touchstones in religion are the tools religious institutions employ either to develop or to maintain a sense of authority, something we all seek in various ways, whether from medical experts, financial advisors, or psychotherapists.

Seeking an authoritative voice in all of these areas, including religion, responds to a deep need in each of us for a sense of safety and security in an increasingly complex and often violent world. We may freely admit, for example, that psychotherapists are fallible, just like everyone else. But that's not the reason we seek their therapeutic insights. And we would certainly prefer medical advice from someone who is more than just a "liminal" physician. The need for religious authority resonates even deeper as religion tries to deal with such ultimate issues as our place and role in the universe and the meaning of life itself. For ultimate questions, we quite naturally seek authoritative answers. For this reason, religious institutions can easily abuse their authority by promising what they cannot in fact deliver.

The profound mysteries of human life, no less than divine life, provoke the kind of questions for which simple answers are not merely inadequate but also offensive and even insulting. With that danger in view, both those who ask and those who try to answer religious questions might consider revising their expectations. Rather than safety, genuine authority in religious matters should prepare for us the inevitable vulnerability we experience when dealing with the deepest mysteries of being alive and human. Rather than the known and the familiar, true religious authority points to the unexplored and the strange. Rather than speaking with certainty, an authentically authoritative religious voice speaks courageously and with the willingness to risk being wrong. This kind of religious authority runs throughout the stories we read in the Bible, in the experiences of Abraham and Moses, Miriam and Ruth, Solomon and David, in the lives of Mary, Elizabeth, Joseph, and John the Baptist, to name just a few. For each of them, dancing with God proved surprising and risky. It exposed them to derision and ridicule and launched them on life-changing adventures they probably would not have chosen to take but later couldn't imagine choosing otherwise.

Constructing a theological method from this kind of religious faith means much more than dealing with things like creeds, catechisms, and liturgies. While those texts are undeniably helpful, they mark only the beginning, rather than the end, of a religious journey. Anglican Christians find that the most fruitful (if not the most comfortable) approach to the life of faith springs from the hope inspired by fallible conversation partners crafting common prayer in an adventure still unfolding and taking some surprising turns. For Anglicans, religious authority emerges not from the answers given to questions but in the process of shared, faithful inquiry.[3]

The four ways to practice hope suggested here overlap and interact. They work in concert, not as a way to define Anglican Christianity within a set of precise parameters, but as a way to talk about how Anglican theologies offer assistance in surprising encounters with Divine Reality. And these encounters will surprise us when we realize the depths of the divine desire from which they come and the lengths to which that desire will go to reach us. Remember, one of the truest things we can say about reality is this: God desires us. Whether we realize it fully or not, this God of desire and of love invites us to dance. And whether we hear the divine music or not, it plays continually, all around us. It doesn't matter at all whether we feel ready to dance or feel sure of the steps, because others will help us. When we stumble on that dance floor, as Christians have done and will do, God will keep playing the music and provide ways to dance better the next time. That is the hope of Christian faith to which Christian theology seeks to bear witness.

Anglican Christians try to put Christian hope into practice by creating communities of genuine conversation where we expect our lives will be changed and in which we learn to welcome the richly textured gifts of a widely diverse human family. Giving an account of this hope, which theologians try to do, can prove no less daunting than putting it into practice, which Anglican communities try to do. In either case, living with this hope takes faith and, as Anglican Christians have realized rather acutely, Christian faith demands a great deal of courage.

2

THE DANCE FLOOR
~ An Invitation to Courageous Faith ~

An empty dance floor is both inviting and daunting. The first time I walked into a dance studio, the polished oak floors and the open, uncluttered space spoke clearly to the care and attentiveness of the instructor. The studio itself seemed to vibrate with the energy of all those who had learned to dance there before. The gleaming floor, both warm and stark, issued a silent invitation, like a blank canvas calling to an artist or a clean piece of white paper urging you to pick up a pencil.

Writers, painters, and dancers all know the thrill of this kind of invitation—and the anxiety that comes with it. The blank paper or the blinking cursor of a word processor challenges the writer to craft the perfect sentence. Even the smallest stretched canvas can look vast before brushing on the first stroke of color. An empty dance floor can make us question the flexibility of our joints and the grace of our muscles.

Viewed from the edges, a dance floor teaming with dancers can create just as much anxiety as an empty studio. For me, the only redeeming quality of high school dances was the punch bowl. Constantly refilling my glass with punch gave me an excuse for not asking anyone out to the dance floor, where I would probably look awkward and foolish. Hovering on the sidelines of the dance felt much safer to me than plunging into the mass of gyrating bodies. At the same time, my sideline hovering was tinged with wistfulness.

My classmates certainly appeared to be enjoying themselves and I could feel the music's rhythm working its magic on my bones and muscles, but I was afraid of going out on the floor and getting it wrong.

Dancing with God requires courage, the willingness to step out on the dance floor even if it means looking foolish now and then. In more traditional terms, dancing takes faith. While it's certainly possible to study Christian traditions without it, it's virtually impossible to put that theology into practice apart from the foundation of faith. What such a foundation really looks like, however, deserves careful attention. Whether it's the image of a crowded high school dance or an empty dance studio, the dance floor itself, with its wide open, beckoning space, always evokes for me two insights about Christian faith. First, the opposite of faith isn't doubt; the opposite of faith is fear. Second, faith doesn't mean living with certainty; faith provides the courage to live with hope.

I encountered these two insights in new ways when I joined the Episcopal Church and tried to put Anglican styles of Christian faith into practice. Living with diverse interpretations of the Bible, for example, even in a single congregation, caused some consternation at first. While I expected to hear something different about the Bible after becoming an Episcopalian, I didn't expect to hear multiple interpretations of a single text. Over time, as I participated in lively discussions and witnessed people (even clergy) change their minds about a particular text, I came to see how doubt can actually enhance the life of faith. Participating in a variety of liturgical styles and sensibilities, even in a single diocese, likewise gave me pause. As a newcomer to formal liturgical structure, I assumed there was one proper way to conduct worship. Observing how Episcopalians managed to live and pray together with divergent approaches to liturgy led me to reevaluate what "being right" really means in religious contexts.

These insights about the dynamics of faith began to crystallize in a new way when I enrolled in a jazz dance class. Taking formal instruction in something that would be, at best, a hobby or a form of recreation describes a key aspect of my personality. I want to learn about an activity (preferably by reading a book) before actually trying it. So my fascination with dancing led rather naturally to enrolling in a class where I could learn at least one style properly and formally; I learned quite a bit more from that experience than I expected. I didn't expect, for example, that we would start dancing in the very first class session. This is probably an obvious expectation to harbor about a dance class, but I was startled by it. As someone who actually reads instruction manuals before trying to operate anything, from a coffee maker to a VCR, I thought we might spend at least the first class session learning about the theory of jazz dancing or maybe watching a video. This was, after all, a class for beginners. Instead, following the lead of the instructor, we jumped right in and started learning basic jazz steps by doing them.

Walking onto that dance studio floor required the kind of courage I hadn't realized I possessed, the willingness to look a bit silly and to start dancing when I had virtually no idea of what I was doing. Christian faith involves the same kind of courage, and not just for beginners or newcomers or recent converts. The life of faith perpetually invites us away from the punch bowl and onto the dance floor, where we find both novices and instructors trying new as well as familiar steps. But no matter who's out there on the floor or how well they happen to dance, the dance floor remains constant, even in widely diverse settings. The dance floor is faith.

Anglican Christians are generally willing to dance even when we're unsure of the steps. This doesn't necessarily feel comfortable and there's no guarantee that it will produce a graceful dance. Yet over time Anglican Christians have come to trust that the dance floor of faith will support us, even in our uncertainty. Treating faith as a matter of courage rather than of certainty marks one of the key features of Anglican sensibilities. It lends a peculiar flavor to the kind of hope Anglicans try to practice and a particular rhythm to the way Anglicans do theology. Anglicans didn't invent this understanding of faith, and it's not merely the result of an idiosyncratic Anglican history. Christian communities have embraced and struggled with these dynamics of faith from the beginning, since the Gospels were first committed to parchment. Anglican Christians have, however, made those dynamics explicit by entertaining a healthy dose of doubt in our life together, which also contributes to the kind of theology that emerges from Anglican contexts.

BEFRIENDING DOUBT ON THE DANCE FLOOR

It is one thing to trust that the dance floor will support our weight. It is quite another to believe we will dance well once we step on it. Just like a dance floor, Christian theology invites us into a life where doubt does not destroy faith; to the contrary, doubt keeps faith fresh and lively.

This wasn't the invitation I heard in the religious tradition of my childhood. In that tradition, doubt was the primary enemy to overcome. Making a public affirmation of faith was one of the ways we waged our battle against doubt, especially in what we referred to as "altar calls." These were occasions in our worship services to respond to the preacher's invitation to accept Jesus Christ as one's own personal Lord and Savior. At the moment of invitation, those who wished to do so stood up, moved forward to the front of the church, and stood with the pastor, who would then pray with each person to become a Christian.

I responded to those altar calls many times, which actually misses the point of what was transpiring in that moment. We were supposed to understand our response to an altar call as a life-changing experience of conversion from which there was no turning back. I, on the other hand, continually feared it hadn't really "took." I felt something like an Easter egg dipped in watery dye. The color just slid off the slick shell and, instead of a vibrant red or deep purple, I never managed to absorb more than pale pastels. Doubt made my shell slippery.

I found these altar calls particularly piercing and irresistible when our pastor talked about how little faith is required for this moment of conversion to happen. I was haunted by the image used by Jesus in the Gospel of Matthew, which the pastor frequently evoked on those occasions: "If you have faith the size of a mustard seed," our pastor would say, "you can move mountains" (see Matthew 17:20). It didn't matter that I had no idea how big a mustard seed really is; I felt certain you'd need a microscope to see my faith. So with Jesus' words ringing in my ears I would find myself standing up, yet again, and moving forward for that day's altar call, hoping that this time the Christian dye would stick. My fear of doubt, in other words, had swollen from a molehill to a mountain and I saw no way to move it.

This stands in rather stark contrast to how faith operates in many of the stories from the gospels. Mark's gospel, for example, begins with striking confidence: "The beginning of the good news of Jesus Christ, the Son of God" (1:1). Mark ends quite differently, however, with three women running away in fear from an empty tomb (16:8). In between the first and the last chapters, Mark's gospel paints a picture of confused disciples who are never quite sure what Jesus is trying to teach them. Throughout these encounters, Mark gives us an extended lesson on faith, the enemy of which is not doubt, but fear.

Consider the stories stitched together in Mark's fifth chapter. There we read the story of a man named Jairus, a leader in the local synagogue who comes to Jesus for help. Jairus's daughter is close to death and he begs Jesus to come with him and heal his daughter. While Jesus agrees, this soon seems for naught; word comes that Jairus's daughter has died. At this poignant moment Jesus says something rather curious to Jairus: "Do not fear, only believe" (5:36).

Well, what has fear got to do with it? His daughter has already died. What more was there to fear? Why didn't Jesus say, "Do not *doubt*, only believe"?

In the middle of this story about Jairus, Mark inserts a story about a woman with an unstoppable hemorrhage. As Jesus and Jairus are talking, this woman manages to slip into the crowd gathered around them and touch the hem of Jesus' garments. Jesus turns to her and says, "Daughter, your faith has made you well" (5:34).

Well, what kind of faith does Mark's Jesus mean? Did this woman have absolutely no doubts about what she was doing? Maybe so, but I doubt it. What this woman did took courage, and for Mark, faith and courage work as synonyms. In that first-century culture, a woman with a hemorrhage was considered ritually unclean, as was anyone who came into contact with her. She took an unprecedented risk just appearing in public, not to mention moving through crowds of people to touch Jesus. "Daughter," Mark's Jesus seems to say, "your *courage* has made you well."

Perhaps Mark inserted this story about a courageous woman so he could make a similar point about Jairus. Gospel writers sometimes do that—they let one story interpret another one. In this case, it's important to remember that Jairus was a leader in the local synagogue, a point Mark makes not once but four times in this short story. Prior to this, Mark describes the way in which the religious leadership in that society was lining up against Jesus, trying to trap him, accuse him, and label him a blasphemer. In this story, Jairus, one of those religious leaders, falls down at Jesus' feet, pleads with Jesus for help, and invites Jesus into his home. It took a great deal of courage for Jairus to break ranks with his fellow clergy, just as it took remarkable courage for that woman with a hemorrhage to venture outside of her house. When his daughter dies and the risk Jairus took seems for naught, Jesus says exactly what Jairus needs to hear: "Do not fear, only believe."

Have as many doubts as you want, Jesus says. Just don't be afraid.

Mark makes this point throughout his gospel, contrasting faith with fear, not doubt. As storm-tossed waters fill the boat where Jesus sleeps, as Jesus walks across stormy waters, as Jesus is transfigured on a mountaintop, as Jesus casts out demons, and finally, as women run away from an empty tomb, the disciples are not necessarily filled with doubt, but they are scared out of their wits. The good news Mark offers in each case is always some version of what Jesus says to his disciples after walking calmly across stormy waters: "Take heart, it is I; do not be afraid" (Mark 6:50).

This is, of course, easier said than done. It's one thing for Jesus to say it and quite another to make our hearts stop pounding and our palms stop sweating and actually live a courageous life of faith. Still, reading the gospels as an antidote to fear rather than a lecture on the evils of doubt can change your life. I still present myself for multiple altar calls, as most Episcopalians do every Sunday when we receive Communion. But why I do it makes all the difference in the world. Rather than berating myself for having doubts, I stand at that altar surrounded by those who love me and say, "I'm still feeling kind of scared." Saying that out loud to people who love you can go a long way toward dispelling fear, even in the midst of doubt.

Doubt doesn't destroy faith. Doubt makes faith necessary. Without doubt, we'd have no reason to make a leap of faith. Fear, on the other hand, keeps us glued to our chairs or hunkered down by the punch bowl, paralyzed by how risky everything seems, immobilized by the prospect of looking foolish on the dance floor.

Scientists often recognize the value of doubt better and more quickly than people of religious faith. This has to do, in part, with how our language has developed in contemporary English-speaking societies. The words knowledge, certainty, faith, and belief all tend to work as synonyms in popular culture, as if these words all mean the same thing. To know something is pretty much the same as believing something and to know something with certainty is more or less just like having faith in something. Christian theology, on the other hand, treats these various concepts a bit differently and seeks to clarify the distinctions between them. Making those distinctions can help us move away from the punch bowl and join the dance, especially if we're still afraid of doubt.

When I have achieved a particular level of knowledge in technology—for example, I know how to operate my VCR and DVD players—I know what's required to make those gadgets work with just a flip of the switch or by pushing a button. Depending on my level of technological expertise, I can say I know those things with certainty. Yet this is quite different from the kind of knowledge I have of my friends. Most of us learn soon enough to be wary of saying we know our friends or our spouses in the same we know our technology gadgets. A friend of mine who has been married for more than twenty-five years once remarked to me that his wife became more not less mysterious the longer they were married. The word "knowledge" doesn't work quite as well in that context as it does with machines and appliances.

By the same token, I don't really believe in something called gravity. When I step out of my house in the morning, I don't need any faith at all that I won't fly off into the atmosphere. Gravity is something we all experience simply as a given of our human existence from the moment of birth. Someone might come along and explain to me how gravity works and why I'm firmly rooted on this planet and that explanation might give me a working knowledge of gravity, but it's not going to change how I stroll down the sidewalk.

When we say we know something, we can close the book and be done with it. We simply know it. But when we believe something, there's always just a bit of doubt that goes with it. Rather than closing the book and being done with it, that little bit of doubt keeps us exploring and engaging and experimenting and asking questions and investigating.

That's how scientists have been doing their work for a very long time. Scientists are usually quite reluctant to say they know something with certainty. More likely, they will say they believe something is the case but they need to do more experiments or need more data to be sure. It's that little hint of doubt that has enabled scientists to make truly remarkable discoveries about how the world works. Doubt leads them to further investigation. Just as importantly, the spark of doubt creates a community of investigators who work together on the question at hand and who must either confirm or reject the conclusions.

Belief is a much more lively enterprise than knowledge, precisely because it involves faith rather than certainty. When we're certain about something, there's no longer any need to ask further questions; the matter is settled. Faith, on the other hand, always has more questions to ask, it's more dynamic, more forward looking, and more engaging. More than that, and especially in Anglican contexts, faith creates a community of seekers and askers and investigators, a community in which each us can say, "Friends, I'm still feeling a bit scared here," yet step out on the dance floor anyway.

The attempt to purge oneself of doubt rarely succeeds. Befriending doubt rather than trying to eradicate it energizes the life of faith and reminds us why we need the company of other dancers in living that life. Befriending doubt also gives a particular shape to the choreography the dance floor of faith invites us to learn. If faith means living with courage rather with than certainty, Christian theology will likewise exhibit a bit less precision than many people probably expect. This lack of precision becomes particularly evident after spending some time with Anglican Christians on the dance floor.

ANGLICAN CHOREOGRAPHY

The dance floor beckons. We might doubt our ability to dance gracefully and we might be unsure of the steps, but the dance floor calls to us nonetheless: Do not be afraid. We might find the courage to take that step on our own, but surrounding ourselves with other dancers greatly enhances our willingness to do so. Each of us might harbor some doubts about how to dance, but taking that step with others can quickly quell the fear.

Even then, stepping on the dance floor, doubts and all, is just the beginning of the life of faith. After taking that step, a host of factors suddenly come into play for the actual dance: the type of music, the underlying rhythm, the other dancers on the dance floor, the dynamic exchanges and negotiations of both movement and space encountered with the other dancers, and the steps for the dance itself. These are just some of the things theology is supposed to help us understand and to do.

In this sense, theology functions as the choreography for the dance of faith. Yet as most dancers realize, a particular choreographic model usually looks a bit different in practice than it does on paper or in the mind of the choreographer, a difference that is often a function of the particular skills and body types of the dancers. Even a single set of dance steps looks different in the hands of different choreographers. The discipline of theology exhibits the same kind of diversity. This discipline has been approached and configured in remarkably different ways throughout Christian history. There has never been just one Christian theology, not even in the Bible. Just as types of dances vary, so do types of theological reflection, each with its own tempo and particular rhythms. In the midst of this diversity, beneath it and supporting it, is the foundation of faith, the dance floor of our life with God. The dynamics of faith, however, also apply to theology: Theological reflection takes courage.

The anxiety and even fear each of us experiences at the prospect of stepping on the dance floor, even if we have done so many times in the past, can tempt us to make of theology something more than it can actually deliver. Some people conflate faith and knowledge and try to make of theology a kind of textbook on God. Others mistake confidence for certainty and try to make theology an argument rather than an invitation. These temptations are particularly potent in my own life as someone who prefers to know exactly what I'm doing before I do it, especially if I'm going to do something in front of other people; I want to get things right and I don't want to look foolish.

Religion typically provides a way to organize an otherwise messy world. It can give us a map for negotiating the complexities of human life and relationships, offer a sense of security about how the world operates and our place and role in the world. But to suppose there might be various ways and not just one way to organize the world around us, or to realize that our religious map depicts not only superhighways but also two-lane country roads, can create profound anxiety. Imagine stepping foot on a dance floor after studying and practicing the steps for a waltz and the band strikes up the music for a rumba, a dance you've never studied. The dance floor is exactly the same one on which you learned to waltz, but now you're disoriented by the rhythms of a rumba, unsure of how to move your feet, suddenly plagued by doubts and probably by the fear of looking foolish. Yet the dance floor and the music and the other dancers all beckon you to dance nonetheless. Dancing with theology often feels exactly like that.

The academic discipline of theology developed over the course of many centuries as a way to give us some idea of what to do after stepping foot on the dance floor. These instructions for the dance eventually crystallized into a traditional pattern and then diversified into the theological specialties students encounter in seminaries today. While pastoral theologians study congregational dynamics and spiritual formation, moral theologians deal with the process of making ethical choices. Historical theologians study the development of Christian doctrines in their various cultural and social contexts while systematic theologians, sometimes referred to as dogmatic theologians, try to organize the breadth of Christian ideas into a comprehensive system of thought. In each case, theologians try to soothe the anxiety of stepping foot on the dance floor by providing instruction in what to do when we take that step.

The desire to provide ever clearer and more detailed instructions for theological dancing has led systematic theologians, like those in the other theological specialties, to diversify their field of study even further, into sub-specialties. Each of these divisions of expertise has expanded considerably in the modern era: Ideas and concepts about Jesus are considered with reference to Christology; notions of salvation are examined with reference to soteriology (from the Greek verb *soter*, which means to rescue or to save); exploring what we mean by the Holy Spirit is worked out in pneumatology (from the Greek word *pneuma*, which can mean either wind or spirit); the dynamics and purposes of church are worked out in ecclesiology; and the mysteries of life after death, the Second Coming of Christ, and the "end of the world" are grouped together in eschatology (from the Greek word for "last things"). Presumably and ideally, each of these subspecialties works in concert with all the others to form a coherent system. In this sense, systematic theology is like an Arthur Murray dance school, which prepares its students not merely to waltz or two-step, but to feel comfortable on the dance floor with nearly any kind of music.

Anglican theologies, by contrast, have not relied as heavily on this impulse to build systems or to provide systematic instruction for the dance. This doesn't mean Anglicans care less about coherence and academic rigor than either our Catholic or Protestant counterparts. Indeed, Anglicans turn regularly to the insights from each of the theological specialties. It does mean, however, that Anglicans have recognized the fluidity and occasional spontaneity of dancing with God for which systems cannot always adequately prepare us; not even Arthur Murray instructors are willing to claim perfect dancing proficiency among their students. While these fluid lines in Anglican theologies emerged as much by historical accident as by intentional design, Anglicans have nonetheless discerned some theological insights in those historical quirks.

The development of theology as a rigorous discipline of study emerged in tandem with European universities. In fact, the medieval concept of theology as the "queen of the sciences" provided much of the impetus for constructing a university system. Over time, however, with the impact of modern scientific method and the development of secular nation-states on the European continent, theologians felt compelled to defend theological study as a legitimate system of thought, to make theology just as worthy of academic investigation as physics or biology. In part, this led to the complex and intricately constructed systems of theology that historian of medieval philosophy Etienne Gilson once described as "cathedrals of the mind."

The cultural and political situation in England, however, looked decidedly different. The bond between church and state in Great Britain, still evident today, did not occasion the same kind of systematic scrutiny of theology. Instead, the development of theology in the Church of England and in English universities gravitated more toward historical inquiry and responded to particular and occasional questions of public concern rather than to the impulse or the necessity to build comprehensive systems.

There have been and continue to be important exceptions to this characterization of Anglican theologies. From Richard Hooker in the sixteenth century to John Macquarrie in the twentieth, as well as contemporary figures such as Mark McIntosh and Rowan Williams, more typically systematic constructions of theological ideas do occasionally appear in Anglican contexts, and often quite fruitfully. Yet even then, these theological constructions do not usually appeal either to traditional systematic foundations (such as Thomistic thought in Roman Catholicism) or to commonly shared confessional statements (such as the Augsburg Confession in Lutheranism).[1]

The differences between English and continental European approaches to theology contributed to the diversity of Anglican theologies with which our seventeenth-century forebears struggled no less than Anglicans do today in our twenty-first-century global communion. Historically, some Anglicans preferred to draw on the insights of Protestant reformers, which evolved into the Evangelical wing of the Church of England. English Evangelicals like Charles Simeon and William Wilberforce led the charge to abolish slavery in the British empire (well before the American Civil War) and to lobby for more humane conditions among the working poor. Others tried to incorporate explicitly Catholic sensibilities in Anglican contexts, such as those involved in the nineteenth-century Oxford Movement. John Keble and John Henry Newman typify this "high church" movement, which dealt equally with elaborate liturgical ceremonial and a retrieval of early church doctrinal formulations. Still others, like F. D. Maurice, also in the nineteenth century, were attracted to the insights of "liberal Protestantism," which relied less on traditional doctrines and turned more explicitly to the ethical teachings of Jesus as a model for social reform.

William Temple, in the twentieth century, insisted on listening to each of these theological voices, arguing that we cannot afford to reject any of them. Truth, Temple recognized, cannot be captured in a single system but will emerge only in a concert of voices and in the ongoing struggle to create harmonious chords from their singing. To put this in another way, the dance floor of faith invites us at times to waltz and at other times to rumba and at still others to a free-form hoedown. In each generation, this Anglican approach to theology poses slightly different questions yet operates with the same kind of courage—the courage to step out on the dance floor even when we're not sure what kind of music will play next. Equally important for Anglican theologies is the willingness to learn new steps from the other dancers encountered on the dance floor.

In John's gospel, Jesus tried to prepare his disciples for precisely this kind of challenge. "I still have many things to say to you," he says, "but you cannot bear them now. When the Spirit of truth comes, he will guide you into all the truth . . . and he will declare to you the things that are to come" (16:12–13). Notice that Jesus didn't give his disciples a timetable. He didn't say, for example, "Two years from now you will have learned all the steps you will need for the dance." Even after Pentecost, when the "Spirit of truth" moved dramatically and explicitly in and among the disciples (Acts 2:1–13), those early Christian communities kept lurching their way toward truth, struggling to discern exactly where and how God was leading them. The writers of these early Christian texts are evoking an ancient insight about Divine Reality of the sort found in Isaiah: "Thus says the Lord," Isaiah writes, "I am about to do a new thing . . . do you not perceive it?" (43:16, 19); and again, "I am about to create new heavens and a new earth" (65:17). These are rather astonishing claims for religious writers to make about Divine Reality, especially if religion is supposed to be essentially conservative and traditional. These images are repeated in the Christian scriptures as well, as in the Revelation to John: "And the one who was seated on the throne said, 'See, I am making all things new'" (21:5).

Anglican theologians take these images and claims to heart, not by abandoning the past, nor by trying to preserve theological traditions in their original or "pristine" condition. Rather, Anglicans take historical traditions seriously by bringing them into creative conversation with the new things God is perpetually bringing about. System building can take us only so far in this constantly evolving dance, which Matthew's Jesus tries to describe in the image of a wise householder. Every scribe trained in the things of God, Jesus says to his disciples, is like a householder who brings out of the treasure chest that which is both old and new (13:52).

Anglicans likewise recognize—though not without considerable consternation at times—just how untidy and tenuous this kind of theological work can be. It is not always clear how the past ought to inform the present. Embracing the new things God brings about can call various aspects of theological traditions into question, even some of the most cherished moments of religious history. Jesus tried to prepare his listeners for this as well by reminding them what can happen when new wine is poured into old wineskins—before long, the old skins will burst (Matthew 9:17; Mark 2:22; Luke 5:37). The long history of Christian traditions exhibits this ongoing and dynamic tension between the old and the new, which never quite resolves itself. The foundation of faith—our dance floor—invites us to find ever better ways to dance with the old steps.

Anglican styles of Christian theology dance on the foundation of faith, not with systematic knowledge or by appealing to certainty but as the practice of hope. Confident in the dance steps provided by historical traditions, Anglicans nevertheless expect the occasional unfamiliar rhythm and creative innovation in the music when we step foot on the dance floor. But we step out on the dance floor anyway, willing to look foolish, surrounded by others who will take the leap with us, and trusting we'll learn from our missteps.

At the same time, the loose threads and untidy edges of Anglican Christianity make Anglicans particularly prone to charges of muddleheaded thinking, or that Anglicans can never quite manage to dance gracefully or even consistently. The desire to learn new steps and respond to innovative rhythms can make Anglicans look tentative, or like dilettantes, or awkward and gangly, like teenagers moving only haltingly away from the punch bowl toward the dance floor. Even for committed Anglicans, the dance floor can feel far less secure than it ought to be. Some long for a more solid place to stand, grounded more surely in scripture or in the strands of a clearly consistent and historically unbroken tradition.[2]

Historically, the longing for a more secure foundation in Anglican theologies has never been successfully satisfied; the attempts always fail. But this does not mean Anglicans live without a faithful place to stand. Anglican Christians do indeed live with such a place and we stand there each and every Sunday morning. Gathering regularly around the eucharistic table to share with each other a simple meal of bread and wine perpetually renews the foundation of our faith, not with certainty but with hope. It is upon this foundation that we can learn best how to dance with the God who makes all things new.

A EUCHARISTIC DANCE FLOOR

Parsing the intricacies of academic theology, comprehending the subtleties of systematic coherence, and negotiating multiple theological approaches in Anglican Christianity require lots of energy and hard work. Sustaining a commitment to sorting through let alone digesting so many texts and creeds and catechisms in Christian history can seem a bit overwhelming. The dance floor of faith can look crowded and the dance itself too complex or academically challenging to join. The dance floor will sometimes look like the exclusive domain of instructors and experts or like mastery of the steps is required before joining the dance. Anglican liturgies can perpetuate these assumptions, as any first-time visitor to an Episcopal church will likely admit. Juggling a service leaflet, a Prayer Book, at least one hymnal (usually two) while simultaneously figuring out when to stand, sit, kneel, and bow requires quite a commitment from everyone, but especially from a newcomer.

Whether with reference to theological traditions or liturgical complexities, it's easy to lose sight of the invitation issued by the dance floor. Faith invites us to dance, to dance with the God of abundant life who yearns to see us thrive. Issuing this invitation is the fundamental intent and task of even the most densely written theological text or the most highly choreographed liturgy. While exploring those texts and rites—from a desire to dance better, perhaps, or to understand why others are dancing a bit differently— the instructions can sometimes trump the dance itself. Fascination or frustration with the intricately woven steps can even obscure the dance floor. It is then we need especially to remember the point of doing theology in the first place.

At their best, theologians don't seek to categorize God or to define precisely what encounters with Divine Reality look like. If they do, and there are plenty of examples of this attempt, they betray one of the key insights of Christian faith: God cannot be contained in our categories. Rather than offering definitions, theology issues an invitation to participate in the mystery of Divine Reality. "Mystery" in this sense is not a puzzle to solve but a life to live. The discipline of theology should help us live that life, not by answering all of our questions and solving the puzzle, but by inspiring the courage to dance.

The doctrines of Christian theology aren't ends in themselves. When they are understood that way, they can quickly become a spiritual litmus test to determine the degree of one's "orthodoxy." Instead, the doctrinal formulations of theology point beyond themselves to the God who continually makes all things new, to the hope of what God has yet to accomplish among us and in us and throughout the world. Rather than argued positions to which we must give our assent, theological doctrines can spur our thinking, entice us to explore, push us to ponder the insights of our ancestors, and give voice to a mystery. Speaking about a mystery won't necessarily explain it, but it just might invite us deeper into it.

Consider, for example, the experience of reading a love sonnet. The poetry points to the experience of falling in love and, if the poet is particularly well skilled, it might even inspire love, but the sonnet is not the love itself. Moreover, one's own experiences with love are never quite the same as anyone else's, and while my loving relationship might bear some resemblance to love's description in the sonnet, it will not be precisely the same.

Or consider the hard work it takes to maintain a healthy marriage. An essay in *Psychology Today* about the dynamics of human relationships or the advice of a family therapist can help keep a marriage on track. The essay and the therapy are helpful and sometimes indispensable tools, but they can never substitute for the actual work of being in a relationship with another person. Moreover, neither the essay nor the therapist can say exactly what it's like to be in one's own unique marriage. Even when we're on the inside of a loving relationship, there is always still more to discover, more to learn, and more to understand. In this way, marriage becomes less like knowing someone and more like delving deeper into a mystery.

Or return to the image of dancing. The studio instructor can tell you how to move your feet for a waltz or a two-step. The instructor can even demonstrate the steps. The actual experience of dancing, however, and managing the idiosyncrasies of your own body and muscles and responding to the equally unique movements of your partner, always feels and looks slightly different from how the instructor described it.

Christian theological traditions function in much the same way. They can describe encounters with Divine Reality, they can provide instructions for trying to dance in those encounters, and they can even demonstrate what that kind of dancing looks like in particular situations. These things are helpful and even essential, but they are no substitute for the encounter itself, for actually dancing with God, which will look and feel slightly different from how the traditions describe it. And just like falling in love, working on a marriage, or practicing dance steps, Christian faith continually inspires us to "get things right." We want to treat the beloved well when we fall in love. We want to nurture a healthy and thriving marriage. We want not merely to dance well but also gracefully. Christian faith likewise moves us to find ever better ways to dance, to learn the difference between good and bad theology, and to discern exactly how it is God intends us to live. It inspires us to make decisions about our conduct of life based on what we believe about Divine Reality. This is what Anglicans try to do by keeping theology securely connected to ethics.

Not coincidentally, engaging in Anglican approaches to ethics proves no less daunting than describing Anglican theologies. The characteristically Anglican willingness to step on the dance floor without knowing precisely how to dance informs not only Anglican theologies but also Anglican approaches to ethics. This is not so surprising when we remember that the word "ethics" derives from the Greek word *ethos*, which refers to the characteristic traits and typical modes of behavior exhibited by a community or an institution. Ethos refers to a group's habitual way of being in the world, how we relate to and interact with the world around us. It describes the daily and constant process of making countless decisions—some of them automatic, some deliberate—about our conduct of life. Christian ethics perpetually invites us to ponder how we are living now and how we should be living, a mode of inquiry that depends on some understanding of who we are as God's people. The theological ethos among Anglicans, however, would not seem to prepare us very well for making those kinds of choices.

Rather than systems of thought, Anglican theologies rely on something more akin to a historical smorgasbord. Anglican theologians typically respond strategically and practically to particular problems when they arise and borrow theological ideas from various historical traditions when appropriate. This hardly seems sufficient, however, for a secure and confident place to stand when making complex and vexing ethical decisions. Ideally, sustained reflection on Divine Reality should be firmly linked to decisions about our conduct of life: Appropriate action requires deliberate thinking; disciplined practice demands well-honed ideas; faithful decisions spring from a decisive faith. To paraphrase Matthew's Jesus, we need a place to stand built on rock, not on shifting sand (7:24–27).

According to the caricatures of Anglican Christianity, Anglicans don't have any such rock-solid place to stand. Anglicans actually appear to avoid such a place, perhaps for fear of giving offense (we do tend to favor polite and civilized discourse), or because we worry that our loosely constructed and significantly diverse worldwide communion will finally crumble if we do take a stand. I'm often reminded of these perceptions and quandaries when fielding questions from newcomers to Anglican traditions.

"What do Anglicans believe about abortion?" an inquirer might ask.

"Well, that depends on the circumstances," I might say.

"Okay, then what do you believe about Jesus?"

"Well, that depends on how you understand the history of the tradition and how our creedal statements developed in their particular contexts."

"I see," says the inquirer, increasingly dubious at the prospect of actually receiving an answer. "So what's your position on divorce and remarriage, on the authority of the Bible, on transubstantiation, on capital punishment, on same-sex blessings?"

"Well," comes the well-worn reply, "that depends."

Needless to say, "that depends" does not play very well in a culture devoted to sound bites and slogans. Nor does it offer a compelling vision for a decisive Christian faith. On the other hand, "that depends" can function as shorthand for what Anglican Christians ultimately do wish to say about both theology and ethics. And what Anglicans want to say about such things is based on what we learn in our liturgical life, in our life of common prayer.

Turning to liturgical celebrations of the Eucharist will not give us quick and definitive answers to life's perplexing questions. More than a few of today's ethical debates clearly harbor expectations for that kind of resolution. Understandably, many people begin ethical reflection by asking whether something is "right" or "wrong." The answer seems obvious for issues like stealing and lying. But is stealing bread to feed a starving child always and undeniably wrong? Could telling a lie to protect a friend from harm ever be considered the right thing to do? Taking contextual circumstances into account when making ethical decisions highlights the importance of doing both theology and ethics with others, the importance of sustaining genuine conversation in a community of faith. The untidy edges of those communal engagements require both courage and patience. They won't produce a clear map for the road ahead or an instruction manual to consult when the process breaks down—but they will inspire hope.

Some Christians prefer to avoid those complexities by turning the Bible into a rulebook and understanding Jesus as primarily a teacher of ethics.

Frankly, I'm often perplexed when people talk about Jesus as a "good teacher." By today's standards, Jesus would seem to fall short of good teaching. He wasn't always patient with his "students." He frequently spoke in riddles and puzzles, and his exhortations don't sound like very practical advice: Lose your life in order to find it; love your enemies; give no thought to your bodily needs; sell all of your possessions; if your hand offends you, cut it off; hate your father and mother; rejoice when you're persecuted; turn the other cheek (so it can be slapped too). I fail to see how any one could put each of those teachings into daily practice.

Problems will always occur in treating Jesus as a teacher of morality whenever his teachings are abstracted from the larger gospel story of his life, death, resurrection, and the gift of the Holy Spirit. In popular parlance today, Christians stumble in their ethical decisions by asking, "What would Jesus do?" They stumble over that question when they fail to consider what Jesus has *already* done. The gospels are not only about what Jesus taught; they are also and mostly about how Jesus gave himself away, for the sake of love and abundant life. According to the gospel writers, that's what God is like.

Every celebration of the Eucharist is a reminder of God's own self-giving in love, which reorients ethical questions quite dramatically. Rather than asking whether a particular act is right or wrong, celebrating the Eucharist prompts a set of deeper questions: If this is who God is, then what kind of person should I be? What kind of priorities ought my life to have? What kind of community is being shaped by this kind of God? How should such a community live in the world?

As people formed by participation in eucharistic liturgy, Anglicans remain suspicious of propositional statements as answers to theological and ethical questions. "That depends," we want to say to such questions, "on the story of God's own self-giving in love." Whether with reference to the divine act of creation, or to the people of Israel as God's own beloved, or to the life, death, and resurrection of Jesus and the animating presence of the Holy Spirit, the eucharistic story recounts the ongoing offering of God's own self for the sake of abundant life. Over time, that story shapes a peculiar kind of people.

The eucharistic story is not a story about rules, though we will find ourselves wanting to create some as we hear it. It's not a story based on analytical principles, though we will want to use some to help us understand it better. This is not a story with a code of conduct attached at the end, like a moral at the end of one of Aesop's fables. This is the story of God's own self-giving in love, which can likewise inspire us to give ourselves away for the sake of love and abundant life. From this perspective, addressing questions of ethics ultimately depends on what it looks like to give oneself away for the sake of love in a particular context and with reference to particular circumstances.

The eucharistic table provides Anglicans with a "place to stand," a dance floor of faith, but not because it offers certainty. To the contrary, being shaped by the eucharistic story actually involves a great deal of risk. Rather than certainty or perfect clarity of vision or even agreement with each other, the story of God's own self-giving in love gives us the courage to do the same with our own lives, even when we're unsure of the form such self-giving will take. Anglicans are not the only ones who stand at the eucharistic table, but we are particularly well poised to show others how to stand there courageously. At that table, we join the dance without knowing precisely where the choreography will lead us.

To be molded by the eucharistic story means we are people who have doubts but who are no longer afraid to take risks. We can risk giving ourselves away in love because the story reminds us that love is even stronger than death. We can risk bold choices in our conduct of life because even in our moral failures the story promises forgiveness and reconciliation. We can risk new ideas and experiment with diversity and welcome the stranger because the story pushes us to imagine God's realm of grace as much larger than we now realize and to admit that our sense of communal identity is probably too small. We can risk making the sharpest critique of even the most cherished social conventions, we can risk standing up to the most powerful institutions and corrupt governments, because our dignity and even our sense of safety and security do not depend on the state, or on our socioeconomic status in society, or even on being correct. All of this depends instead on the community shaped by God's own self-giving in love.

The eucharistic table is our courageous place to stand as Anglican Christians, not with certain knowledge but with a hopeful faith. On such a dance floor, we can begin to explore in more detail the particular steps Christian faith invites us to practice in dancing with God. For there are steps to learn for this dance, even if it takes a lifetime to learn them and even if, as Anglicans are wont to do, we resist defining the steps with precision. A good place to begin this exploration is by looking more closely at what we mean by the word "God" and how our language about Divine Reality can either help or hinder us in learning the choreography of faith. The exploration begins, in other words, with the divine music we hear on the dance floor.

3

HEARING THE MUSIC
~ The Trinitarian Rhythms of Christian Faith ~

My godson recently celebrated his second birthday. As a first-time god-parent, I have been taking great delight in watching Louis move through his developmental stages from infant to toddler. His language skills are just now starting to accelerate (with words like "no," "mine," and "momma") but he's been mobile and walking for some time. In watching Louis I have found it intriguing to discover that body and muscle coordination for mobility develops well before complex linguistic skills. Given how much time adults spend talking compared to walking, one might suppose the order in which these skills develop would be reversed. This is clearly not the case. In fact, it wasn't long after Louis managed to stand upright on his own that he also started to dance. To be sure, he's not ready to audition for the Joffrey Ballet. Nonetheless, flip on the stereo, play some music, and his tiny body auto-matically responds to the rhythm.

Where did this impulse to dance come from? Louis's parents certainly don't spend their time dancing around the house. With two children to care for and another one on the way in a household menagerie of two dogs and two cats, they don't have the time (and certainly not the energy) to dance. If Louis's tentative attempts to dance aren't merely imitations of his parents, some other kind of link must be operating between music and muscles, as if rhythm and movement are hard-wired in our motor skills. Coordinating body movement into recognizable dance steps clearly requires more than muscular intuition. For both professional and amateur dancers, those skills take time and practice. Still, even those who never dream of stepping foot on a dance floor can recognize distinctions in tempo and rhythm. Even those with supposedly "two left feet" can hear the difference between a waltz and disco. Louis clearly knows rhythm is for movement, even though he can't even speak those words yet.

I grew up in a distinctly non-dancing household and attended a private Christian college where social dancing was forbidden. As most parents realize sooner or later, forbidding something only makes it more attractive. So, not surprisingly, almost immediately upon graduating from college, I headed for a dance club. With no formal dancing instruction to speak of, I made sure to surround myself with good friends who wouldn't laugh (at least not overtly) at my fumbling attempts to dance. Both to my surprise and delight, dancing came quite naturally. I don't mean I have a natural talent for dancing well. I mean only that by listening to the music I could feel the rhythm in my muscles urging me to move and to dance. Since then, I have been an enthusiastic observer of dance and occasionally a student when I want to coordinate my muscles more intentionally and in a particular way.

Bridging the gap between an instinctual muscular response to music and training those muscles to perform gracefully requires both patience and commitment; the music itself inspires that kind of work. Likewise, the distance between my godson's halting attempts to move his body rhythmically and my attempts to learn the fox-trot, though seemingly vast, is really just a matter of time and physical development; both Louis and I are simply responding to the music. We can say something similar about believing in God and about encounters with Divine Reality.

Put aside for the moment all the complex philosophical, cultural, and religious arguments for God's existence. Peel away the many layers of human reflection on what the word "God" really means, those many centuries of ritual and prayer and the many texts, manuals, and catechisms for learning appropriate religious dance steps. Beneath them all is divine music, as familiar to us as the rhythm of our breathing and the tempo of our beating hearts. Just being alive and drawing breath can put us in touch with profound mystery. The fact that I might not have existed at all sometimes reminds me that my life itself is pure gift. Knowing what to do with that gift, however, and knowing where it came from involves much more. These are ancient quandaries from which a host of philosophies, religious traditions, and spiritual disciplines have developed to address the meaning of life itself and what we ought to do with this mysterious and amazing gift called life.

Encounters with Divine Reality almost always exhibit this strange mix of the completely natural and the extraordinarily complex. It's one thing for Louis to move his two-year-old muscles to music and quite another to waltz gracefully with a partner. The distance between those skills is bridged by the music, which will sound different to Louis as he grows older, even if it's exactly the same song. Likewise, it's one thing to stand in awe of the sheer gift and mystery of life, of simply being alive, and quite another to know what to do with this gift, to know how to live. The distance here is bridged by the Giver of the gift, the Source of the music of life.

Life itself is the divine music playing everywhere and all around us, but we sometimes have trouble hearing it, as if straining to discern a forgotten melody. At times its distinct rhythms rise up from our daily routine, urging us to move our muscles, enticing us to learn some dance steps. Mostly, this divine music plays in the background of our lives, audible but slightly muffled. I can hear the music from my stereo when I'm doing housework, but the drone of the vacuum cleaner makes it mushy. Just as my godson will need to train his muscles if he wants to dance a proper waltz, each of us needs to train our ears to hear divine music and then learn how to dance to it. This is what theology can help us to do.

The many doctrines, creeds, and rituals of a religious institution don't create the divine music of life. At their best, they train our ears to hear it and offer us a way to coordinate our muscles to its rhythm. In Christian faith and theology, this divine music appears in the rhythms and cadences of Trinitarian language, building on the traditional notes of "Father, Son, and Holy Spirit." How these rhythms create the music of life remains a profound mystery to which our theological traditions can only point with the hope of inspiring us to dance. Theology, in other words, is not the music itself. Even in its most complex formulations, theology is simply a response to the mysterious music of Divine Reality. And when the theological invitation no longer inspires us to dance, theologians seek fresh ways to describe divine music with the hope of hearing it more clearly.

The task of refreshing theological language infuses religious traditions in countless ways, from the earliest forms of Israelite religion forged in the crucible of desert wanderings to the clarion call of the Hebrew prophets, from the wide array of images for Jesus used by four distinct gospel writers to the many schools of Christian thought that developed in the centuries that followed. In this sense, a religious institution functions like a repertory ballet company. The history of visionary choreographers and composers provides the tools for new dancers to hear the rhythmic subtleties of music. Working together, they learn how to express that music with their bodies. Meanwhile, the company's artistic director searches through the many documents and commentaries on past performances, gleaning insights and imagining improvements while taking into account the particular talents of the dancers at hand. Christian communities work in much the same way as we dig into historical traditions for clues about divine music and advice for how to dance to it.

Each era and every generation faces its own unique quandaries and opportunities in discerning how the divine music invites us to dance; yet the music itself continues to play. Christian theology invites us to hear that music as Trinitarian, for which the traditional language of Father, Son, and Holy Spirit is only one possible description. Naming this mystery has never been easy or free from controversy. The complexities of Trinitarian language (which a friend of mine likes to describe as "bad math") would seem only to confound our attempts to speak clearly about Christian faith as good news, and for many reasons. Referring to God as "Father," for example, provokes concerns about gendered language and the way religious concepts shape social and cultural dynamics. A masculine divinity can quickly make masculinity itself divine. The qualities and character of parental relationships likewise vary from culture to culture, making the language of "Father and Son" vulnerable to potentially unintended meanings and connotations. Even the word "persons" with reference to the Trinity raises questions about modern notions of personhood compared to ancient cultural assumptions. These and many other factors contribute to the complexity of giving voice to Trinitarian mystery.[1]

As Christians today experiment with various ways to speak of the Holy Trinity, the goal in such experimentation has remained the same since the earliest Christian communities first composed a gospel: To hear the divine music as clearly as we can. Anglican Christians insist on hearing this music in a wide range of locations and not just in our church buildings or from our pipe organs. What we do and say and what we hear in church expresses in a particular way the divine melodies running throughout human life. We can hear it in the arts and culture, in scientific inquiry and investigation, in loving relationships and the creation of families, and in the astonishing beauty of the created world around us. Anglicans have likewise recognized the importance of listening for this music together, of learning the rhythms of the divine dance in the company of other dancers, both historical and contemporary. Just as my godson instinctively feels the rhythm of music in his muscles, I instinctively gathered friends around me for my first trip to a dance club. Without question, each us can hear the divine music, but to hear it clearly and to dance well, we need help. This is one of the fundamental insights of a Trinitarian faith: Encountering Divine Reality creates a community, because Divine Reality is not only personal, but also essentially social.

Anglican theologies create a healthy amount of space for experimenting with various ways to speak about God, each of which reflects the dynamic character of Divine Reality. As encounters with Divine Reality usually demonstrate, God refuses to stay put in our systems of thought. Anglican approaches to theology likewise insist on speaking about Divine Reality not as an object of study but in terms of relationship, which we do not merely analyze but in which we "live and move and have our being" (Acts 17:28). This then is the challenge Christians have always faced and for which Anglican Christians already possess some helpful tools to address today: How do we find language for that Reality in which and by which our every breath depends? What kind of language about this Reality can move us to live with hope, both for ourselves and for the world? How do we speak of traditional Trinitarian faith as an invitation to abundant life?

Addressing these questions first begins, as many theologies do, with the image of God as Creator. Yet this doesn't say enough if we fail to see every act of creation as a self-offering of the Creator, just as composers offer something of themselves in every piece of music they write. Christians wish to say even more, as the divine composer not only writes the music but also plays it and dances to it. A Trinitarian faith pushes us still further to see ourselves caught up in the music and participating in this divine dance. Our participation in the dance is the hope to which Christian theology has tried to point by speaking of Divine Reality as Trinitarian.

At the same time, the desire to give voice to the mystery we call God carries significant risk. Trying to speak clearly about the divine music of life can quickly lead to explanations, which never quite suffice for talking about mystery. Many of the roadblocks in adopting a Trinitarian faith come from this desire and from the need human beings have to explain things. There's certainly nothing wrong with that desire; perpetual human curiosity leads us to explore and inquire and make some remarkable discoveries about how the world works. But explanations can take us only so far.

Consider the complexities of human behavior and the idiosyncrasies of human relationships. The tools of psychology, sociology, and anthropology can go a long way toward explaining those human dynamics, but they eventually run headlong into a wall of mystery. This can happen even when we try to explain our own lives to our friends. As Archbishop of Canterbury Rowan Williams has observed, human beings turn to metaphorical and even paradoxical language quite frequently to speak about the mysteries of their own lives. We do this, Williams notes,

> because even in banal contexts, we are aware of the fact that our pigeonholes for things, people, emotions, and perceptions are often lagging well behind the fluidity of the real world, with its subtle, rapid interactions and its puzzling quality. And whether it is in theoretical physics or in poetry, we need to express some sense of this strange fact that our language doesn't "keep up" with the multiplicity and interrelatedness and elusiveness of truth.[2]

If human beings have trouble speaking clearly about our own lives, how much more so when we try to explain divine life? If we can explain something, we're more likely to think we can control it, or worse, we take it for granted as something that's no longer very interesting. And what we mean by the word "God" ought to be at least interesting if not endlessly fascinating. Maybe that's why Jesus preferred to speak in parables rather than explanations. The metaphorical and analogical language of parables invites us to break free from precise definitions and use our imagination, which is a far better tool than explanations when trying to speak about mystery.

Christian traditions have at times tried to explain Divine Reality, but less frequently than many people probably realize. Christian history actually offers not just one way but many ways to speak about the rhythms of Trinitarian mystery and none of them turns out to be entirely adequate. Taking that history to heart, Anglican Christians have insisted on retaining the Trinitarian character of Christian faith even while experimenting with new and imaginative ways to speak about it. This process of experimentation has continued for centuries, which can caution us against trying to find the ultimately correct formula for Divine Reality. Rather than speaking correctly, Christian faith continually invites us to speak better and for the sake of inspiring the hope to which a Trinitarian theology tries to point: To hear the divine music of the divine dancer and at last to join the divine dance itself.[3]

For Anglican Christians, putting this Trinitarian hope into practice is just as important as trying to describe it. The history of Trinitarian descriptions continues to play a significant role in the life of faith for Anglicans today, but Anglicans rely just as much on the Trinitarian rhythms of conversation and conversion encountered in thriving, diverse communities of faith. Living with these rhythms will not lead to perfect words or formulas. Ultimately they lead to worship, where we discover, both joyfully and maybe with considerable surprise, that proper language no longer matters. The journey into this mystery begins with hearing its music.

THE DIVINE COMPOSER

Taking piano lessons as a child prompted a series of insights for me. I found it both fascinating and challenging to learn the system of musical notation and how to link the printed marks on a page to their corresponding keys on a keyboard. After mastering those rudimentary skills, my piano teacher insisted on telling me something about each of the composers whose music I was learning how to play. At first, this seemed like a distraction from the task of actually learning a new piece of music. Over time, I came to see its worth and value.

Every piece of music contains traces of the composer. To play a piece of music well, and not just adequately, it helps to know something about who wrote it, the historical era in which it was written, and the cultural background and personal circumstances of the composer's life. On a written score, I came to realize, composers leave traces of their hopes and dreams, their fears and failings, their joys and loves, all of which begin to appear vibrantly when the music is played and we can hear some of the echoes of the composer's inner life. Traces of the composer's life appear even more clearly when the music invites us to dance. By dancing to a piece of music, we not only hear the composer's presence, we also begin to feel that presence in our bones and muscles.

To speak of God as Creator in some way evokes these insights about musical composition. Whether we stand in awe of the Swiss Alps or the Grand Canyon, whether we ponder the vast expanse of our solar system or the seemingly endless reach of oceans, whether we tend carefully to a bed of iris, play with a golden retriever, or cradle a newborn baby in our arms, each of these moments is a strain of divine music and each contains a trace of the divine composer. Just as a Beethoven symphony or a Count Basie jazz riff offers something of either Beethoven or Count Basie himself, so the divine creation offers something of God's own self.

The book of Genesis, in the opening chapters of the Bible, has been one of the traditional places to read about this divine creativity. It provides the score, as it were, for the divine music playing all around us and in us. Yet the classic images from Genesis sometimes tempt us to locate divine creativity in the distant past, as if the divine composer wrote only one piece of music. If, on the other hand, we see in creation an offering of God's own self, as Genesis invites us to do, then the work of the divine composer has not yet come to an end.

Consider those now famous opening verses of Genesis. The story begins, not with nothing, but with the chaos of discordant notes and unformed melodies. Merely by speaking, the divine composer draws harmonious chords from the chaos, creating light and dark, sun and moon and stars. Merely by speaking, the divine composer creates the rhythms of plants and animals, of trees and grasses, of fish and birds. At long last, this music of life gives rise to a composition more closely resembling the composer. As the storyteller in Genesis puts it, God creates humanity in God's own image.

Here the storyteller sounds a remarkable note. "It is not good," God says, "that the man should be alone" (2:18). Remarkable, because until this point in the story everything about the divine composition has been declared not only good but *very* good. Remarkable, because this creature, who ought not to be alone, is created in the image of the Creator. Divine creativity, in other words, springs from God's own desire for communion and companionship. The divine composer longs for dance partners, and the music of life is God's invitation to dance.

In learning to speak adequately about this Divine Reality, we quickly discover the limits of human speech. How much can we presume to know and therefore to speak about a composer based solely on the composer's music? That question points to the problem of language, of trying to capture dynamic rhythms and haunting melodies in words or on paper. The difficulties only deepen when we try to describe the fluid motion of a dance.

Today, the word "God" hardly suffices for describing Divine Reality and our participation in it. That word has grown thin and vacuous as it gets tossed around rather flippantly in both exclamations and jokes. It has also been distorted by countless layers of cultural and even religious baggage as many people cannot help but imagine Divine Reality as an old man with a flowing white beard. Some actually prefer the familiarity of this image, as it keeps Divine Reality at a relatively safe distance, like a benign monarch reigning beyond the clouds. Biblical writers recognized this problem long before we did and refused to restrict their language about Divine Reality to a single image. For the ancient Israelites, language for Divine Reality included a wide range of possibilities: "strong rock," "safe harbor," "still small voice," "whirlwind," "jealous spouse," "shepherd," and even an "angry she-bear protecting her cubs," to name just a few.

For Moses, speaking adequately about God required a burning bush. Before this encounter, Moses was presumably quite familiar with the music of life as he raised a family and tended his father-in-law's goats. Yet this wasn't quite enough. In the third chapter of Exodus, Moses turns from his mountainside goat tending to investigate a mysterious fire, the flames of which burn but don't consume a bush. He soon recognizes this moment as an explicit encounter with Divine Reality and learns a new way of speaking. This was a moment of conversion for Moses.

At first, the voice Moses hears in that encounter reveals what many people today have come to expect in stories about God. "Come no closer!" the voice says. "Remove the sandals from your feet, for the place on which you are standing is holy ground" (3:5). Appropriately enough, Moses then hides his face. At this point, the story offers the notes of familiar music: The sacred remains distinct from the ordinary; divine glory resides on a remote mountaintop; Divine Reality inspires fear and awe. If the story ended there, Moses would not have learned anything particularly new. But the voice continued.

"I have observed the misery of my people who are in Egypt. . . . I know their sufferings, and I have come down to deliver them from the Egyptians" (3:7–8). Now this is new. To speak adequately about Divine Reality means speaking not only about the composer of life's music. We must also speak about the composer who becomes involved in how the music is played. This alone would have sufficed as a life-changing moment for Moses, who had fled Egypt in fear for his life and settled into the simple contentment of goat herding. But there was still more to learn; the voice continued.

"So come, I will send you to Pharaoh to bring my people, the Israelites, out of Egypt" (3:10). Moses is dumbfounded and actually objects, as I suspect many of us would. After all, who are we to do or even say anything about God's own music of life? The story in Genesis provides the answer to that question: We are created in the image of the composer. To us God has entrusted the divine music, and with that music comes the desire to play it well so that all may dance to its life-giving rhythms.

To speak of divine creativity means speaking of the energy springing from the depths of God's own desire for abundant life and which continually moves the Creator to become involved in how the creation unfolds. The composer cares how the music is played and yearns to see all of us dance to it. Hearing the music of this divine desire as traces of God's own self among us compels Christians to venture saying something more. A Trinitarian Christian faith moves us to speak of Divine Reality not only as the composer of life's music, but also as the dancer.

THE DIVINE DANCER

The ancient Greeks were not only philosophers. They were also accomplished mathematicians and astronomers, which is stating the case rather mildly. Centuries before Columbus stumbled upon a new continent, the Greeks had already realized our planet is round and were able to determine its circumference with remarkable accuracy. They did so by observing the angles of the shadows cast by the sun and using the geometric calculations school children still learn today.

The beauty and harmony of mathematical astronomy led one of those ancient Greeks, Pythagoras, to describe the inner workings of the universe as the "music of the spheres." His philosophic colleagues, a bit less adept at poetic speech, preferred the Greek word *logos* to describe virtually the same thing. *Logos* means "reason" or "word" and deals with notions of rational discourse. Thus, for the ancient Greeks, both *logos* and "music of the spheres" described the principal of orderly design in the universe, the glue that holds the whole thing together.

Early Christian writers seized on these ideas to make an astonishing claim: The music of the spheres danced among human beings in the person of Jesus. The first chapter of John's gospel makes this connection explicit. "In the beginning," John's gospel says, "was the word (*logos*)," through whom all things were made, and this word became human flesh. The word God speaks in Genesis, the melodies of that divine voice bringing forth the rhythms of life, this same word dwelt among us, "full of grace and truth" (1:14). Here the dance of God's self-offering in the music of creation intensifies. Just as God creates a companion in God's own image, and as God urges Moses to the work of liberation for the sake of life, as God calls a particular people as God's own beloved, so this same God, John's gospel seems to say, enters the dance of human life itself.

To speak of Divine Reality in this way stretches the limits of language. It doesn't fit well into the rational discourse the Greeks envisioned as the only way to speak about the universe. It doesn't admit careful parsing or precise calculation or logical analysis. The gospel writers knew this, yet they persisted in making their claim: We have encountered Divine Reality in Jesus, no less than Moses did in a burning bush.

Still, the gospel writers seemed to struggle with how to speak adequately about this encounter. Matthew, Mark, and Luke each put a slightly different spin on the same story and these three differ, sometimes significantly, from John's approach. Each of them experiments with new ways to speak about Divine Reality for which their language, they realized, did not have precisely the best tools. The gospel writers employed a variety of images and titles for Jesus—Son of God, Son of David, teacher, prophet, bread of life, the Good Shepherd, and so on—but Jesus himself often comes across as rather cagey about his own identity. Jesus certainly appears to act as only God would— healing diseases, forgiving sins, and even raising the dead. But there's no record of Jesus ever explaining to his disciples that God consists in the unity of three persons and that he was the incarnation of one of those persons. That kind of theological language emerged much later, developed after sustained reflection on the clues, hints, and frequently poetic speech of the biblical writers. Explicitly Trinitarian language certainly finds echoes in the Christian scriptures, but even the Apostle Paul needed to ponder what it really means to speak of God as "three-in-one."

We can link biblical authors and later theologians by noting the impulse they shared to stretch the limits of human language, to find a way to speak about the mystery of God and our participation in that mystery. In part, the way in which these early communities found themselves moved to pray and to worship sparked this desire to clarify their speaking. Praying to Jesus and in the name of Jesus as if Jesus were God, or experiencing the presence of what they came to call the Holy Spirit among them as if this presence were also God, eventually raised some vexing questions about how they ought to speak about Divine Reality.

Christians have always worried about speaking properly in matters of faith and theology. At times, they tried to articulate proper Christian speech for the sake of securing a particular position of power in the institutional church, but just as often they did so for the sake of making Christian faith a matter of good news. Over time, the anxiety about language generated distinctions between "heretical" and "orthodox" Christian speech, or the distinctions between improper and proper ways of speaking about God. Yet even then, what was considered orthodox took on a variety of forms and employed a rather wide range of images and metaphors and analogies.[4] Throughout this long theological conversation, which continues to this day, at least this much remains constant: Encountering Jesus prompts new ways to speak about Divine Reality, which Christian traditions came to describe as the Holy Trinity.

The language of ancient Christian thinkers may not translate well into twenty-first-century cultures, but there's still much to learn from their attempts to shape Christian speaking and living. The diversity of those ancient attempts serves as a reminder that there's not just one way to speak about Divine Reality; there are many. This doesn't mean that every possible way to speak about God is adequate or helpful. It does mean that theological traditions offer a bit more room for conversation than many contemporary Christians probably realize.

Anglican theologies, more firmly rooted in historical investigation than in doctrinal systems, embrace the expansive quality of Christian traditions as a way to invite further conversation about the good news of God-in-Christ. The willingness to embrace conversation, even with reference to what we mean by the word "God," springs in part from appreciating the developmental character of Christian thought. Christian theology did not suddenly appear, whole and complete, from the gospel writers. Christian theological ideas evolved slowly and over the course of many centuries, punctuated equally by moments of temporary consensus and widely divergent opinion. It's actually difficult to imagine theology transpiring in any other way when we pause to realize how tongue-tied we can become when holding a newborn infant in our arms or when gazing across a vast ocean. In moments such as those, language either fails us or we resort to poetic speech. Finding agreement on how to speak about such experiences is quite beside the point—but the desire to speak persists. So it is with the history of theological traditions, the history of finding words for Divine Reality.

Listening carefully to historical conversations has been one of the key features in Anglican Christianity, but not for the sake of defining precisely what the word "God" really and finally means. Rather, listening to historical conversations offers important help in making Christian theology an explicit invitation to dance. Among those many conversations, three points of historical contact emerge as particularly illustrative of both the diversity of Christian traditions and the opportunities for finding fresh ways to speak about the good news of a Trinitarian faith.

The first point of contact comes from the fourth-century reflections of Augustine, one of the classic shapers of ancient Christian traditions. By this time in the history of Christian thought, difficult questions had emerged about the kind of God Christians claimed to worship. Describing Divine Reality as Trinitarian raised questions, for example, about divine unity. Are we in fact worshipping three distinct Gods by the names of Father, Son, and Holy Spirit?

Augustine, who influenced the Western, or Latin trajectory of Christian thought, said no. There are not three Gods, he said, but one, and he located their unity in a single divine "substance" shared equally among the three persons. Finding ways to speak adequately about this Trinitarian insight, however, continually eluded him. For a time Augustine seemed keen on talking about the Trinity as "the Lover, the Beloved and the Love that binds them together." While this image had potential, Augustine worried about explicitly erotic imagery for God and decided to abandon this language as inadequate. He then turned to something like psychological introspection for Trinitarian language. After all, if humanity is created in the divine image, each of us must bear traces of that Trinitarian reality. From that insight, Augustine experimented with language derived from reflecting on his own interior life and proposed several approaches, mostly variations on the triadic pattern of "memory, understanding and will." Even here, Augustine realized that these insights, while helpful, don't quite capture the mystery of divine life.

The second point of contact comes from a group of three theologians known collectively as the Cappadocians (named after the place of their birth): Basil the Great, Bishop of Caesarea; Gregory, Bishop of Nazianzus; and Gregory, Bishop of Nyssa. These theologians influenced the Eastern or Greek trajectory in Christian thought and, while they offered their work at roughly the same time as Augustine, they addressed the question of divine unity slightly differently. Rather than a single divine "substance," they located the unity of God in the mutuality of the relationships the three persons shared. This, they believed, offered a better way to speak about Divine Reality as essentially social, an indispensable point of contact for Trinitarian faith. Although they never said so explicitly, the Cappadocians also seemed to worry about the traditional language for God they had inherited. To speak of "Father, Son, and Holy Spirit," they realized, implied relations of power and subordination, which put at risk the mutuality of relationship they hoped to articulate.

The third point of contact emerged several centuries later, from the eighth-century work of John of Damascus. John appreciated both the Augustinian and Cappadocian approaches yet tried to expand and deepen their insights. The Cappadocian anxiety about language and the relations of power led John to explore more carefully the Greek concept of *perichoresis* as a way to describe Trinitarian reality. This Greek concept has been notoriously difficult to translate adequately into English. It evokes a sense of permeation without confusion, encompassment without circumscription, penetration without violation. Even better, some have discerned in this Greek word a hint of the English word "choreography," the dynamism and vitality of which John of Damascus wished to apply to the Trinitarian persons of God. More specifically, John was articulating a sense of fluid partnership in which there are neither leaders nor followers but only an eternal movement of shared giving and receiving. From this perspective, to speak of God as three *persons* is not really adequate at all; we must instead speak of three *dancers*, the mutual and eternal choreography of which makes it impossible to discern the dancers from the dance itself. And the dance is nothing less than creative self-giving love.

For many Christians today even this brief foray into the history of Trinitarian doctrine confuses rather than clarifies what we mean by the word God. Many would also find language about "divine substance" and even "shared relationality" fairly remote from the routine of day-to-day life. Anglicans appreciate the historical points of contact in these theological traditions but also recognize their limits. Merely studying these ancient traditions can never substitute for the experiences and encounters to which those traditions try to bear witness.

In their attempts to speak about Divine Reality, theologians usually have a twofold purpose in mind. They want to give voice, as best they can, to the insights gleaned from encounters with God. They also want to lead others into similar encounters where some of the same but also some new insights will likely occur. Encounters with Divine Reality never look or feel exactly the same, and they depend on the particular community, culture, and historical era in which they occur and from which the language to describe them is taken.

The history of these encounters and how Christian communities have tried to speak about them offer plenty of clues and insights but not a precise or detailed map for our own encounters today. Augustine, the Cappadocians, and John of Damascus would all insist they were speaking about the very same Divine Reality, but each of them chose a slightly different way to map their insights. Each of them would also insist that the point of theology is not the map but the encounter and actually to live a Trinitarian faith. Like dancing, we can learn just as much by putting Christian hope into practice as from reading theological texts about it. Like Trinitarian theology, the point of learning the choreography is to join the dance. For Anglicans, this intersection of thinking and doing offers the most compelling point of contact for embracing a Trinitarian Christian faith and for discerning why such a faith offers genuinely good news: To speak of the Holy Trinity is to issue an invitation into the divine dance of abundant life.[5]

THE DIVINE DANCE

To speak of joining the divine dance of life evokes a long and often complex history of theological speculation in which Christians have often found it easier to say what God is not than to say what or who God really is. And this is precisely how it should be. If theologians were able to capture and categorize exactly the meaning of Divine Reality, they would no longer be talking about God. Theological language deals in mystery, not definitional precision. Unlike the plot of a mystery novel, however, the divine mystery is not something ultimately to solve but something to live, a profound hope to put into practice. None of this, however, makes theological language irrelevant—far from it.

Language is a powerful tool in shaping and interpreting human experience. It's one of the key ways human beings discover and create meaning in the mystery of human life and relationships. This is especially so for religious language, in which many people invest a great deal of time and energy. In this sense, theology is never neutral but can either help or hinder the process of trying to put hope into practice. The ways in which Christians speak about encounters with Divine Reality therefore deserve constant vigilance.[6]

Today, linguistic vigilance falls under the banner of "constructive theology," or the work of teasing out a variety of insights from our historical traditions and translating them appropriately into contemporary contexts. Anglicans have been engaged in this kind of theological work for quite some time, which comes with no guarantee of either systematic clarity or even practical certainty. It does, however, come ripe with the hope of fresh and lively insights. As we apply this constructive work to our concepts of God, some of the language Augustine ultimately found problematic can still prove helpful for us today, especially in concert with the insights gleaned from both the Cappadocians and John of Damascus.

In learning to speak adequately about Divine Reality (which is not to say comprehensively or exhaustively), Christians wish to speak of a relational or social reality, for which the language of erotic desire offers some of the best resources. Augustine's reluctance to entertain erotic language for theological insight stemmed in part from his own personal history with sexuality and the particular dynamics of sexual relations at work in his own culture. The Cappadocians' anxiety about relations of power was likewise shaped by the way in which families were constructed in ancient societies. Neither sexual nor familial relations in those cultural contexts aspired to the same kind of mutuality they do today. This presents an opportunity for us to retrieve some of those ancient insights more fruitfully for own contexts, especially with reference to erotic desire.

Eros was one of several ways the ancient Greeks spoke about human desire. Broadly speaking, the erotic refers to the intense longing for communion, for giving ourselves away to another. This desire is usually expressed in terms of human sexuality, yet we need not restrict it to sexual relations. The longing and desire for communion finds expression in any number of ways, through deep friendship, communal bonding, interactions with the environment, and so on. In this sense, ancient Christian thinkers recognized the potential in erotic language (even if they shied away from it) for speaking about God's Trinitarian interaction with the world and with us. This is the language of self-offering, as anyone who has been in love knows so well. When we fall in love, we not only desire the beloved; we also desire to give ourselves to the beloved. In this exchange of desire, love itself emerges as something more than just the sum of the lover and the beloved; love reveals itself as the "third" in this dual exchange.[7]

For Christians, this dance of desire and self-offering describes the very heart of reality itself, which our ancestors in faith chose to describe as the Holy Trinity. It also led Augustine to experiment, at least briefly, with the language of the Lover and the Beloved to describe God's own life, and the Love itself as the energy of divine creation. Or to borrow from John of Damascus, the music of divine love brings forth creatures in the divine image, inviting those creatures to dance. However we wish to speak about this Divine Reality, a Trinitarian Christian faith compels us to think about Christianity as fundamentally social and participatory. Divine music invites each and every one to the dance of life.

Anglican Christians believe the work of discerning these Trinitarian rhythms transpires best in the company of other dancers. While we need not restrict such musical rhythms to what happens inside our church buildings, Anglicans nonetheless turn to liturgical traditions for reminders of how to listen for divine music in our daily lives—in our work, our recreation, our relationships, and the countless decisions we make concerning our conduct of life. Putting this in another way, Anglicans hear Trinitarian music as communal melodies, inviting us into the divine rhythm of conversation and conversion.

Celebrating the Eucharist together, sharing a simple meal of bread and wine, sounds those communal notes in a particular way. Most eucharistic prayers follow a traditional pattern by recalling the work of God in creation, the calling of Israel as God's own beloved, the life, death, and resurrection of Jesus, and the animating presence of the Holy Spirit in the world around us. Each of these moments of divine music contributes to the story of God's own self-offering, traces of which are made visible in the bread and wine shared around the eucharistic table.

While hearing the music of divine self-offering gives a better sense of the steps for our own dance, it also leads quite naturally to worrying about dancing well, about whether we're dancing correctly and properly to the music. This anxiety can create complex and sometimes rigid systems of ethical rule keeping and rigorous spiritual discipline, as the history of Christian traditions clearly shows. Listening carefully and regularly to eucharistic music, however, shapes that historical impulse a bit differently. Eucharistic music focuses our attention on the dance itself, which our anxiety over the choreography can easily obscure.

Divine music invites us to dance just as God does, to the rhythms of self-offering for the sake of abundant life and loving communion. But the mystery of communion, just like the mystery of the Trinity, isn't something we can engineer, control, or manipulate by adhering to a rule-based spirituality or insisting on categorical definitions for Divine Reality. To be sure, examining our conduct of life and carefully reflecting on our faith can help us appreciate divine music in new ways, in much the same way studying the score of a Beethoven symphony can reveal his compositional genius. At the same time, the score of Beethoven's Ninth pales in comparison to actually hearing it and to the experience of being enveloped by it. In much the same way and over time, eucharistic music draws us into the Divine Mystery. We are lured and enticed there by the deathless, self-giving love of the God who created us and longs for us, as a Lover for the Beloved. Moreover, as we are caught up in this music, we inevitably find ourselves changed by this dance of desire and love. Over time we find ourselves not only willing but eager to give ourselves away for the sake of life, for the sake of inviting others into the dance of God's own abundant life.

Dancing to the music of divine self-offering is the profound hope to which the "score" of Christian theology and ethics tries to point. As many Anglicans have discovered, practicing this hope in the hard work of sustaining genuine conversation and embracing ongoing conversion can create some peculiar communities. The choreography can feel choppy, uneven, and far from polished.

Nearly every Anglican congregation exhibits some degree of diversity in both belief and practice. While some members find traditional language about the Trinity comfortable and inspiring, others trip over it as outdated at best, or worse, a roadblock in their encounters with God. Creating fluid dance steps from these diverse perspectives can stretch the limits of both patience and imagination. In my experience, I've known Episcopalians who are virtually unitarian in their theology but attend church faithfully and give generously of their time and money to food banks and homeless shelters. I've known others who insist on strict definitions of Christian orthodoxy, who worry about receiving Communion with those whose theology they find questionable, and who rarely participate in the congregation's outreach programs. I've known many others who fall somewhere in the vast religious space in between those extremes.

Evaluating these various religious dance steps raises a number of serious concerns. It seems just a bit fussy to question the content of someone's theology when he or she seems to be living a traditional faith in practice. On the other hand, it's not always clear why the practice of someone's faith seems inadequate when the content of her or his theology clearly draws from historical traditions. Besides, who makes all these evaluations and for what purpose? And what ought any of us to do when the evaluations are offered? What role, if any, should "evaluation" and "assessment" play in our unfolding dance with God?

Diversity in Anglican contexts, while not unique, is nonetheless made explicit in the way Anglicans dance together. At times it can inspire us to dance better and, at others, to wonder whether we can and who should decide what constitutes a good dance. Our efforts toward better dancing will likely falter if we insist on just one way to speak of Divine Reality or require mastery of the choreography before stepping foot on the dance floor. Restricting theological speech to a single formula or metaphor actually betrays the insights of a Trinitarian faith: The mystery of Divine Reality cannot be defined or categorized but only described and evoked. By the same token, evaluating theological beliefs apart from the practical consequences of those beliefs fails to appreciate the learning that comes from doing and how insights evolve as they are put into practice.

Anglicans acknowledge all of these complexities but don't simply abandon either theology or ethics as impossible. Instead, Anglicans have learned to trust that theological and ethical insights emerge only from sustained conversation over time. Anglicans certainly did not invent the importance of conversation; Christian communities have always relied on it. Jesus conversed with his disciples. His disciples conversed with their friends and families. The Apostle Paul engaged in prolonged and often heated conversations with the communities he founded and tried to nurture. These conversations continued to spread and, with them, the good news of God-in-Christ. Each of these conversations incorporated theological texts, religious traditions and practices, and the experiences, hopes, and dreams of the particular people involved. Some of these conversations were undoubtedly more akin to sermons

and lectures. Some of them hardly qualify as examples of free-flowing dialogue. Nevertheless, Christian theological and ethical traditions are the prod-
ucts of a continuing process of conversational exchange and debate in which
mistakes and missteps offer as many insights for the dance as moments of
fluid and graceful choreography.

Some theological conversations have only just recently begun, some of
them have been going on for decades, and still others have stopped altogether. Somewhere in our religious history, for example, Christians stopped
having the conversation about whether women should attend church when
they're menstruating, which the Bible clearly forbids. That command
appears in the Levitical holiness code, along with the admonition to stone
disobedient children. The Bible also envisions the ideal of head coverings for
women in church, who ought to keep quiet in worship anyway. Christians
have also stopped talking about usury, the practice of exacting interest when
loaning money, which not so long ago was forbidden in European society
for religious reasons. Imagine if we still insisted on making such a practice
illegal and what that would do to our global economic systems, both for
good and for ill.

Christians have stopped talking about many things, but we're still having
a conversation about others. As Western governments devote more and more
resources to the "war on terrorism," some Christians want to talk about what
Jesus really meant by loving our enemies, which always sounds perplexing if
not unrealistic in times of armed conflict. Parts of the Anglican Communion
are still in conversation over the ordination of women and the ministries of
gay and lesbian people. Some of us have given up on having conversations
about these things, too, which now threaten serious divisions among some
of our Anglican provinces.

Without the faithful art of conversation—whether it's with the Bible,
with our traditions, or with each other—we have no hope for creating the
kind of common life in which we can learn how to dance better. Embracing
this kind of conversational faith casts a different light on the typical carica-
ture of Anglicans as wishy-washy and muddleheaded. The reticence to
respond directly and categorically to either theological or ethical questions
reflects the value Anglicans place on the process of discerning the truth
about a matter rather than reducing such truth to sound bites. No one's
heart is ever really changed by reading a bumper sticker or a slogan on a
poster. Sustaining genuine conversation, however, does inevitably lead to

change and growth, or to what our traditions have called conversion. For Anglicans, this means the willingness to give ourselves away in love, to find ourselves changed by giving ourselves to the dance. To hear Trinitarian music is to hear the rhythms not only of sustained conversation, but also the constant call issuing from that conversation to engage in the work of conversion.

If theological truth can't be reduced to a single formula, by the same token, conversion cannot be reduced to a single act of remorse. Indeed, remorse and repentance often play only minor roles in the process of Christian conversion, which involves understanding our place in the world differently because of the invitation to dance with God. It means a complete reorientation of our priorities because of God's own self-giving in love. Conversion means becoming a new creature, as the Apostle Paul described it (2 Corinthians 5:17), and this doesn't happen overnight. William Temple described conversion in this way:

> We have lowered the term "repentance" into meaning something not very different from remorse. Repentance does not merely mean giving up a bad habit. What it is concerned with is the mind; get a new mind. What mind? To repent is to adopt God's viewpoint in place of your own. There need not be any sorrow about it. In itself, far from being sorrowful, it is the most joyful thing in the world, because when you have done it you have adopted the viewpoint of truth itself, and you are in fellowship with God.[8]

Adopting God's viewpoint in place of our own, as Temple put it, is another way to describe dancing with God, whose music invites us to learn particular kinds of steps. Some of these steps will feel familiar; many others will seem quite strange. Dancing with God involves both types of learning: finding better ways to dance to the old steps and discovering new ways to move our muscles to the music. In either case, Christian faith requires the courage to examine assumptions and revise even the most time-tested opinions if the divine dance seems to require it. How prepared are we to cast doubts on our conduct of life? How willing are we to have our minds and hearts changed about reality? How much are we willing to risk in our hope of dancing with the God of abundant life? Personally, my tolerance for risk is fairly low, which is precisely why I cannot imagine trying to dance with God by myself. I need the help of other dancers. If for nothing else, I need them for the courage to step foot on the dance floor. I need help in hearing the rhythms of Trinitarian music.

The ongoing dance of conversation and conversion creates a particular kind of community, the music for which we hear every time we gather at the eucharistic table. At that table, we hear the music of divine self-offering, an offering that does not depend on our response, our comprehension, or our conduct of life. God perpetually offers God's own self, whether or not we deserve such a gift, whether or not we embrace it with open arms, whether we wind up dancing gracefully to the divine music or stumbling and falling flat on our faces. I can't imagine this kind of unconditional divine self-offering creating anything but a rather peculiar company of dancers.

In a world where affinity groups, political parties, and familial bonds all perpetuate the divisions of humanity into like-minded and conflicting factions, the rhythms of Trinitarian music invite a different kind of communal dance. By dancing together at the eucharistic table, by offering ourselves to that dance whether or not we agree with each other and whether or not we approve of each other's life choices, is to trust that the music will lead all of us, eventually and over time, into a more graceful dance. Putting this hope into practice would surely offer the kind of good news a world of violent divisions longs to hear.

The vision of a rich and deeply textured communal dance is the good news theologians try to evoke when they speak of Divine Reality as Trinitarian. The desire to speak, however, frequently goes hand in hand with the desire to speak *clearly* if not correctly. The same kind of thing happens whenever we try to communicate some extraordinarily good news to others and especially when that good news is about God. The natural desire to communicate can tempt us to explain more than we are able. As biblical stories often illustrate, human explanations of Divine Reality can take us a long way, but only to the brink of speechless wonder where our words actually fail us. More often than not, visions of heavenly worship lead biblical writers to abandon language altogether (Isaiah 6:5) or to speak in way that can sound to us like an experience of drug-induced hallucinations (Revelation 4:1–8). Whether they can no longer speak or choose to speak strangely, biblical writers caught up in divine worship travel well beyond the desire to explain those experiences with precision.

Accounts of dramatic encounters in the Bible are not so different from other kinds of experiences human beings have quite regularly: a newborn baby cradled in our arms, gently rocked into sleep; the intimacy of friendship that can make us feel quite surprisingly desirable; that heart-piercing piece of music, perhaps just a single phrase of the melody, sweeping us off our feet and bringing tears to our eyes. These are not experiences we wish to explain but to relish, and in which to find ourselves blissfully lost. When my two-year-old godson tries to move his muscles to music, I don't imagine he wants to find words for the experience or to hear explanations about where the music comes from. He's simply caught up in the moment and wants to dance.

Theologians eventually recognize something similar about their own theology. After arduous study and painstaking interpretation, their many ideas and concepts ultimately lead them to worship. I don't mean only that their theology leads them to a pew in a church building where they recite officially approved prayers. More than that, it leads them to the brink of that encounter in which they realize that their words no longer matter. When Anglicans fuss and argue over liturgical texts and rites, as we are wont to do, we're not hoping finally to "get it right," as if we could one day capture Divine Reality in our words. It's actually just the opposite: We keep fussing with those texts with the hope that Divine Reality will finally capture *us*, and like biblical writers and theologians before us, we'll be caught up in the unspeakable mystery of life itself.

When John's Jesus promised to send the "Spirit of truth," he didn't say anything about explaining the truth, only that the Spirit would "guide us into all the truth" (John 16:13). Jesus seems to be giving us permission to trust the Spirit's guidance and to use our imaginations as we try to speak about the mystery into which that Spirit will lead us. A faithful and Spirit-guided imagination leads us to explore and experiment with language, to take what we learn from centuries of Christian tradition, pour it into the pot of our own experiences, stir it around, and find creative ways to speak about it—not to explain it, but to issue an invitation to go ever deeper into the mystery.

When I do that, I still find the musings of John of Damascus helpful for imagining what the word "God" really means and invites. I no longer imagine God as a solitary monarch reigning beyond the clouds, but neither do I imagine the Trinity as something like an old man whose dying son leaves his ghost behind to haunt us. Instead, I try to imagine the very heart of reality as dynamic, energetic, and social. I try to imagine Trinitarian traditions pointing to the fluid union of dancers in which we cannot tell the dancers from the dance, and the dance itself is endless, deathless love.

This vision of the Holy Trinity invites me to imagine that the divine act of creation is not yet finished, that the work of salvation is not yet complete, and that we have not yet experienced the fullness of abundant life. We have only stepped foot on the dance floor and the music has only just begun to play. And I try to imagine a world transformed by Christians finding even more creative and compelling ways to speak about the Holy Trinity as the great dance of life, enticing the whole creation into its energetic, communal rhythms. As I try to imagine all these things, I learn to trust in the guidance of that Spirit Jesus promised to send. As the long history of Christian thought suggests, that Spirit will continue to shape and reshape all these ideas, words, and concepts until, at long last, the day comes when all of us are fully caught up in the divine dance, thankfully and joyfully lost in wonder, love, and praise.

Meanwhile, as that day has not yet arrived, there is important work to do. As Moses discovered in his encounter with a burning bush, divine music urges us to dance in very particular ways—perhaps for liberation, or for the freedom from tyranny, or shaping the conditions for abundant life. For Christians, the divine music we hear in Jesus likewise invites us into the incarnate, and therefore frequently messy particularities of human thriving. It is this key aspect of Christian hope, to which Anglican theologies so often turn, which now deserves more careful consideration.

4

HOLY HULA HOOPS
~ Jesus and the Hope for Human Thriving ~

Some years ago now, on my first trip to Hawaii, I had the privilege of witnessing authentic hula dancing, or at least the version of hula dancing presented to tourists. As I listened to the drums and watched the dance unfold, I remember marveling at the seemingly impossible way human hips could move. I had a similar experience watching a traditional Native American "hoop dance." The hoops in these dances symbolize the circle of life, with no beginning and no ending. As the dancer gradually adds more and more hoops to the dance—around wrists, ankles, waist, calves, and forearms—each one represents a different stage of life. Watching these dancers incorporate as few as four and as many as fifty hoops in a single dance made me wonder whether my body could ever be that agile and graceful.

In both situations I suspect my experience was fairly typical for a white, Anglo-American Midwestern male. The way in which my own cultural background had trained my muscles' response to music felt natural and normal, while both the Hawaiian and Native American dances looked unfamiliar and seemed a bit exotic. Of course, neither the hula nor the hoop dancers experience those movements as exotic, but rather as quite familiar, natural, and normal.

Distinguishing various experiences as either "normal" or "exotic" depends entirely on one's own perspective and on the cultural background in which each of us is steeped from the moment of birth. Making these distinctions is in part a function of language and how human beings use language to create general categories of description from the particulars of experience. We group diverse things like apples, cheese, and bread into a general category called "food," but we don't include things like tables and chairs in that category. The physical and the human sciences operate in a similar way by standardizing general expectations and then describing particular exceptions as deviations from the norm. This can be reassuring to New Yorkers if they experience a particularly brutal snowstorm in April, which meteorologists can then describe as "unusual." Applying the same kind of distinction between general expectations and particular exceptions to human beings, however, has been far from reassuring; the creation of categories for race and ethnicity is just one example.

By the beginning of the seventeenth century, the success of European colonialism was being built on the backs of slaves. Europeans justified the mass enslavement of Africans by seeing them not merely as "different," but as particular exceptions to the general category of human. By making European ancestry the standard by which to judge what it means to be human, Africans could be treated as property, as "things" to own and exploit. The same tendency continues today in both explicit and subtle ways. Lurking beneath the history of contentious social policy debates and cultural conflicts in the United States is the stubborn assumption that American culture is generally white, or Caucasian; particular bodies with particular skin colors are the exceptions. In fact, many Caucasian people I know don't consider themselves as having a skin color at all. Color attaches only to the general rule's exception, to "people of color," in other words.

The same dynamic operates in categories for sexuality and gender and started shaping Western cultural assumptions long before the Puritans established New England colonies. Many of us have internalized these assumptions without even realizing it. In a variety of ways, modern Western societies adopted the European male as "standard issue" humanity while women and people of color were treated as deviations from this norm. So while some Hawaiian hula dancers and Native American hoop dancers might think of *me* as in some way exotic, it's actually more politically, socially, and culturally significant that I, as a white person, think of *them* as exotic. From that assumption has sprung the long and brutal history of racism in European and American societies.[1]

These are fairly basic and in some sense even pedestrian reflections on the dynamics of race and ethnicity in American culture. Even so, they made a considerable impact on me, not only when I applied them more intentionally to my own participation in the mechanisms of a racist society but also to my understanding of an incarnate Christian faith. By realizing the inadequacy of speaking generally about American society, I came to realize the same risk in speaking generally about God and Christianity. While dancing with God takes on a variety of forms, the steps are always quite particular. This means, among other things, that the good news of Christian faith is just as challenging as it is comforting; Christianity invites all of us to learn unfamiliar steps. Regardless of the culture in which we were raised, dancing with God will always feel at least a bit strange and slightly exotic now and then. This is so even among lifelong Christians, probably even more so for us given the deeply ingrained assumptions that come with being raised in a Christian household. For me, the challenge and therefore the hope of Christian faith appeared more clearly as I discerned the significance of my own, quite particular body. For me, Christian faith deepened and took on added texture when it invited my particular body into "holy hula hoop" dancing.

I grew up in an era when television censors objected to belly buttons and to married couples sleeping in the same bed. Like many other baby boomers, television sitcoms helped to define my childhood. *I Dream of Jeannie* and *The Dick Van Dyke Show* were two of my favorites. In the former, Barbara Eden played the part of Jeannie, whose otherwise suggestive harem-like costume came with one restriction: It had to cover her navel. In the latter, Dick Van Dyke and Mary Tyler Moore played Rob and Laura Petrie, whose otherwise happy suburban marriage included a bedroom with two twin beds.

While both of these instances of bodily propriety sound quaint and antiquated by today's standards, I found them completely unremarkable in the Midwestern, suburban enclave of my American childhood. There, the social and cultural upheaval of the 1960s passed by me virtually unnoticed, as if it were a parade on the far side of town and I had chosen to stay home and read a book. Until the eighth grade, the only persons of color I remember seeing were in school textbooks or on television, the viewing of which my parents carefully monitored. Neither my mother nor the mothers of any of my childhood friends worked outside of the home. Sex before marriage—let alone pregnancy—was unheard of, and the word "divorce" was whispered if it was spoken at all.

Not surprisingly, given that era and cultural milieu, it never occurred to
me that Jesus had a Middle Eastern face or that he ate the kind of spicy food
I had never tasted or smelled spring rain on desert mountains or lived with
a skin color different from mine. There were no images of Jesus in my home
or in the homes of any of my childhood friends, no icons of his face and certainly not of his body. The only body I fancied Jesus having was the one that
died on a cross. Death was the sole connection I could think to make
between my body and the body of Jesus, yet even this link was tenuous without a crucifix in sight, even in church. Bodies mattered only to the extent
that we eventually left them behind, like Jesus did, to go to a mysteriously
spiritual and disembodied place called heaven.

My perception of bodies changed significantly when I first learned how
to dance and when I joined the Episcopal Church. Even the most firmly
held denial of bodily existence quickly evaporates in a dance. On a dance
floor, there's simply no denying the particularity of one's muscles and bones
and where one's center of gravity actually resides (or that there even is such
a thing). Stepping foot into an Episcopal church, especially in an Anglo-
Catholic parish of "smells and bells," as I did, accomplishes something similar to stepping foot on a dance floor. Bodies matter on Sunday mornings as
we see particular colors, smell the sweet odor of incense, move our muscles
to bow, kneel, and stand, actually touch other bodies in a gesture of peace,
and as we hear astonishing words spoken over bread and wine: This is my
body, this is my *blood*; take and *eat*.

Since that time, an increasing number of icons have graced the walls of
my home. Two in particular serve to remind me that Christian faith makes
no sense without bodies, and not just any body, but particular bodies.
Bodies like mine, bodies like yours.

The first is a traditional icon of Mary and the infant Jesus, a copy of one
of many similar images from the Renaissance. I bought that icon mostly
with Mary in mind, as I had not yet added her image to the collection, and
I didn't pay much attention to the baby Jesus—not, that is, until I actually
hung the icon on my wall. It was then I noticed something quite remarkable: The infant is naked and Mary is pointing to his genitals.

I found this icon astonishing, not because I assumed that Jesus had been
born without genitals, but because this explicitly religious image wouldn't
let me forget it. Now, every time I see it, I remember that speaking theologically of Jesus is to speak of a particular human being whose humanity
is particular in every way.

The second icon comes from one among several contemporary artists who create iconic images from a wide range of multicultural symbols and resources. The one I purchased depicts the resurrected Jesus, but not in any of the disembodied ways I had previously entertained. In this icon, drawn in part from Native American images, Jesus is naked and sitting cross-legged with a drum in his lap and a drumstick poised in one hand. Marks of the crucifixion are still visible on his hands and feet and he's wearing branches, fashioned as something akin to antlers, on his head. His eyes carry a fierce and slightly wild quality, certainly not tame, meek, or mild. Even though I bought this icon some years ago, it can still make my heart race. He's inviting me to dance.

Icons are potent resources for theological reflection precisely because, as the old saying goes, a picture is worth a thousand words. The "words" this contemporary icon speaks likely produce some anxiety for more than a few modern Western Christians today: Jesus' naked body makes his sexuality explicit; some of the imagery comes from "pagan," or at least nontraditional Christian symbols; though resurrected, he is still firmly connected to Earth. These words help to expose at least a few of the firmly entrenched assumptions about Jesus that many people continue to harbor, but not by abandoning Christian traditions. To the contrary, that icon retrieves important aspects of Christian traditions that may have been lost or missed altogether.

By confronting me with a particular and unfamiliar body, that icon reminds me of a key aspect of Christian theology. Jesus poses questions not only about God and who God is, but also about humanity and what an authentic human life really looks like. Both kinds of questions—about God *and* humanity—belong inseparably together in any reflection on Christian faith and practice. And those questions inevitably involve the use of language and how the tendency to generalize can sometimes betray us.

When speaking about Anglican Christianity, for example, we soon realize how difficult it is to do so generally, and we begin to talk about particular Anglicans in particular contexts doing theology in particular ways. The same thing can be said about believing in God. Generalities about Divine Reality eventually fall short of the encounters we wish to describe. Moses experienced this problem with language quite acutely when he stumbled upon a burning bush. When Moses found enough courage to speak, he wanted to know which God was sending him back to his people in Egypt. The divine response was both mysteriously general and historically particular: "Thus you shall say to the Israelites, 'I AM has sent me to you'" (Exodus 3:14), and then the divine voice added quite particularly, "Thus you shall say to the Israelites, 'The Lord, the God of your ancestors, the God of Abraham, the God of Isaac, and the God of Jacob, has sent me to you'" (3:15). The great "I AM" is actually bound up with particular people and their particular histories.

Like Moses, Christians do not believe in God generally. Christian faith is quite particular, rooted and grounded in the particular life of a first-century Palestinian Jew from Nazareth by the name of Jesus. For lifelong Christians, the particularity of this belief may no longer shock or startle, but it should. No less startling than encountering Divine Reality in a burning bush is to have a similar encounter in a particular human being, living in a particular ancient culture and speaking a particular language (not English).

Learning to dance to the music of Jesus inevitably exposes a wide array of unexamined cultural assumptions in much the same way my brief exposure to the Hawaiian hula and Native American hoop dancing uncovered some of my white, Midwestern cultural perspectives, the ones I carry deep in my bones and muscles. Assumptions about Jesus are no less entrenched in the "muscles" of modern Western societies. While Anglican Christians live with just as many of those assumptions as anyone else, Anglican theologies create a bit more breathing space for retrieving fresh insights about this central figure in Christian traditions and for the hope of practicing a genuinely incarnate Christian faith.

Anglicans neither invented nor have we fully appreciated this breathing space Christian traditions afford for reflecting on the significance of Jesus. But Anglicans do make such space explicit by recognizing three interrelated yet distinct ways to engage in that kind of reflection. The first relies on the gospel texts and what we can learn from them about the particular historical figure of Jesus. The second turns to the subsequent centuries of theological reflection in which Christian communities tried to make those particular gospel insights more culturally portable. The third focuses on the life of common prayer around the eucharistic table, where the previous two modes of reflection come together in a weekly celebration of the hope of salvation.

Connecting these three overlapping points of contact shapes the way Anglican Christians typically understand the doctrine of the Incarnation, to which Anglican theologies have so frequently turned. By reflecting on the significance of Jesus in this way, Anglicans try to put our traditional theological method into practice and give each "leg" of the three-legged stool its due: scripture (the particular Jesus), theological traditions (the portable Jesus), and contemporary experience (the eucharistic Jesus). Most Anglicans agree that each of these legs remains important, but how they're connected with each other continues to provoke debate. Questions about the significance of Jesus can spark fierce controversy precisely because they tap into the traditional source of Christian hope and what it looks like to practice that hope. Today, for the sake of a genuinely hopeful Christian faith, it is not enough to connect those three "legs" and create a well-balanced stool. Hope demands more than the wooden legs of a stool; hope wants those legs to dance.

Drawing from the dynamic interactions among scripture, tradition, and experience, Anglican Christians can learn some fresh ways to speak about a traditionally incarnational faith. For religious traditions rooted in notions of incarnation, bodies are not merely incidental to the practice of hope; bodies actually matter. They matter ultimately and not merely temporarily. Bodies matter in Christian faith in the same way they matter in dancing—without them there is no dance.

By reflecting on the wide-ranging implications of the Incarnation, Anglican Christians can expose some of the persistent assumptions about Christian faith operating in contemporary popular culture and in some of our churches. Many Christians and non-Christians alike, for example, restrict the hope of salvation to an otherworldly hope, to the hope of having access to that spiritual and therefore disembodied place called heaven. Traditional views of the Incarnation suggest something broader. Rather than treating salvation as an escape from the particularities of human existence, the choreography we learn from Jesus inspires the hope of precisely the opposite: embracing a genuinely authentic human life in God. Salvation in this sense describes nothing less than the hope for human thriving. Discerning the contours of that hope and what it means to put that hope into practice begins with the gospel writers themselves.

THE PARTICULAR JESUS

We know far less about the historical figure of Jesus than we do about George Washington or Queen Elizabeth I. If Jesus ever wrote anything, those texts did not survive. What we do know about what he said and what he did comes to us from the memories of those closest to him and the stories they told, which were written down much later, after his death and the startling news of resurrection. The challenge in speaking about Jesus is similar to writing a family history. That kind of project leads us to old photo albums (with both clearly identified and anonymous faces), immigration records, interviews with grandparents and, if we're lucky, great-grandparents, and countless family anecdotes told by geographically scattered relatives. These sources provide quite a bit of data to work with, but my own account of the Johnson family history will differ, and sometimes significantly, from my cousin Johnny's account, who continues to live in the same town as my father's brothers and sisters. The gospels offer even less data than that about the life of Jesus and his extended family.

We do, however, know quite a lot about the particular religious, cultural, and political context in which Jesus lived and in which the later accounts about him were written. Apart from those historical particularities, the gospels make virtually no sense. Imagine trying to understand the American Declaration of Independence apart from the history of English colonization; some generally inspiring ideas and concepts might appear in that document, but we'd miss their particular historical impact. We likewise risk missing the significance of the gospels if we abstract them from their particular first-century context of colonization by the Roman Empire. Learning the dance steps of the historical Jesus depends on that particular context, both before and after his death at the hands of Roman soldiers.

The Choreography of Jesus' Ministry

Jesus was born in occupied territory, at a time when the Romans had annexed Palestine as a province of the empire and had crafted a tenuous and often uneasy alliance with Jewish authorities. Each of the provinces in the Roman Empire was governed in a slightly different way, which contributed to the longevity of the empire itself. In Palestine, the Romans made allowances for the practice of the Israelite religion and granted Jewish leaders at least the appearance of wielding governing authority. Herod, for example, who plays a role in the stories of Jesus' birth, fancied himself a king but actually served only at the pleasure of the Roman emperor. This made Herod particularly nervous upon hearing rumors of a messiah's birth in Bethlehem. If these rumors proved accurate, this messiah could threaten Herod's comfortable arrangement with the Roman authorities. Herod's violent response to this supposed threat, recorded in Matthew's gospel, illustrates the precarious quality of this negotiated truce (Matthew 2:1–18).

Jewish authorities, for their part, made their own concessions to keep the peace. They allowed the Romans, for example, to levy a variety of taxes on their people, often collected by the Jews themselves. These tax collectors occasionally collected more than was owed and kept what was left over, which only deepened the resentment of their neighbors. According to the gospel writers, Jesus chose one of these tax collectors, Matthew, as one of his own disciples. This choice surely carried economic ramifications and created some underlying social tensions, just as any discussion of taxes does today.

These and other similar moments in the gospels suggest a key insight about the historical development of Christian faith. Jesus apparently cared less, if at all, about creating a "new religion," what we call Christianity, and far more about revitalizing the religious faith of Israel, which had lost its way in the colonial occupation of the Roman Empire. Placing the ministry and teachings of Jesus in that context helps to explain why the presence of Gentile (non-Jewish) followers of Jesus created such moments of crisis. The first followers of Jesus were, after all, Jewish, just as Jesus was, and they struggled with the idea of extending their mission to Gentiles. So, apparently, did Jesus.

In the seventh chapter of Mark's gospel, after Jesus rebukes his disciples for not understanding their own religious tradition, a Gentile woman of Syrophoenician origins begs Jesus to heal her daughter. At first Jesus refuses, reminding her that food for children (Israel) ought not to be given to dogs (Gentiles). Yes, the woman says, but "even the dogs under the table eat the children's crumbs" (7:28). Hearing this, Jesus relents and the woman's daughter is healed, an encounter in which even Jesus apparently learned something about the reach of his own mission and ministry.

Each of the four gospels echoes this growing tension over the scope of the good news Jesus proclaimed, which led eventually to something like a family feud between the Jewish communities embracing the teachings of Jesus and the Jewish communities that didn't. Now, after many centuries of shameful and tragic Christian anti-Semitism, these historical particularities from the first century demand our attention whenever we read the gospels. Consider, for example, the image of Jesus as the good shepherd in John's gospel and what Jesus says to his disciples. "I have other sheep that do not belong to this fold," he says. "I must bring them also, and they will listen to my voice" (10:16). Today, I suspect most Christians imagine those "other sheep" as non-Christians; Jesus meant non-Jews.

The controversy over including Gentiles serves as just one reminder of gospel particularity, of how the ministry of Jesus attached to the particular hopes and dreams, the particular anxieties and fears of particular people. Discerning not only the scope of Jesus' ministry but also its purpose and content created considerable confusion, which the gospel writers described in various ways. In Mark's gospel, for example, the disciples seem particularly dim-witted and incapable of digesting what Jesus meant by "good news." While the disciples in Matthew and Luke seem a bit more adept at listening—though only just a bit—many of them assumed Jesus would lead an uprising against the Roman occupation. What we now call the "triumphal entry" of Jesus into Jerusalem shortly before his death only fueled these revolutionary hopes. John's gospel, on the other hand, locates the confusion in the escalating conflict between Jesus and the religious leaders in Jerusalem—the "clergy," as it were—who worried not only about antagonizing the Romans but also about the integrity of their religious traditions, which they perceived (either rightly or wrongly) was threatened by the teachings of Jesus.

Meanwhile, as the gospel writers describe it, Jesus goes about the business of overturning a wide array of tables, and not just the ones occupied by moneychangers in the temple (Mark 11:15–17). All sorts of cultural customs and religious assumptions are overturned in what Jesus said and did. He shares meals with prostitutes and tax collectors, the freaks and discarded ones on the edges of that society. He spends time with women and welcomes them as students of religious tradition, which was restricted only to men (Luke 10:42). As far as we know, Jesus remained unmarried and childless, a highly unusual and even scandalous choice in a society constructed on familial relations. In Matthew, when he was told that his mother and brothers were waiting to see him, Jesus brushed aside these biological ties and declared that anyone who does the will of God is his mother, his sisters and brothers (12:50). He even says that those who do not hate their mothers and fathers and their sisters and brothers cannot be his disciples (Luke 14:26). His exhortation to love our neighbors as ourselves may still sound radical today yet are quite mild and even unremarkable compared to the ones so often overlooked: Love your enemies; do not judge others; bless those who curse you; sell all you have, give the money to the poor, and follow me.

So while the disciples fantasize about a revolt against Rome and the clergy fret over proper religious observances, Jesus talks about and demonstrates what he calls the "kingdom of God." Contrary to how I imagined it growing up, the kingdom of God is not a place beyond the clouds where we go after we die. Jesus certainly had plenty of other things to say about our life with God after death, but this isn't one of them. The kingdom of God is a particular and concrete way of being authentically human with each other. For the gospel writers, authentic humanity no longer creates hierarchies of value based on class or social status; women and children are taken just as seriously as men and adults; the idea of family is no longer restricted to marriage and biological procreation; economic justice and freedom from oppression carry as much spiritual weight as religious ritual and disciplined prayer; and the rules of a religious tradition serve human thriving and not the other way around as reconciliation replaces vengeance, forgiveness displaces retribution, and grace overcomes condemnation.

These are just some of the particular and rather peculiar steps for dancing an authentic and thriving human life that Jesus tried to model in his ministry. Now, some two thousand years later, that dance still feels unfamiliar and just a bit exotic, and it should. If we take seriously the first-century particularity of Jesus, dancing with him will disrupt the assumptions of every culture in which the hope of that dance is put into practice. Every culture, no less than first-century Palestinian culture, has yet to embrace fully that abundant life Jesus wished to proclaim and the authentic human thriving to which Jesus tried to point. This stands in rather stark contrast to the more generalized Jesus of my childhood, who lived mostly so that he could die and by his death lead me to that place beyond the clouds.

My childhood view of Jesus was not entirely wrong, just woefully incomplete. What that view lacked I have since tried to embrace with the image of a naked, cross-legged Jesus, who bears the marks of his crucifixion while poised to drum the rhythm of a dance. I keep returning to that particular icon precisely because it disrupts the assumptions I still harbor about the hope of Christian faith. Jesus does not lead us away from but rather toward a genuinely human life, the dance of which he himself lived and into which he continues to invite us. The particular ministry of Jesus certainly pushes us in that direction and, as the gospel writers tried to show, Jesus issued this invitation just as explicitly after he died.

The Choreography of Resurrection

Among the many strange and peculiar things recorded in the gospels, accounts of the resurrection are some of the strangest. These stories don't quite follow a standard plot line. They certainly don't tie up all the loose threads like typical Hollywood screenplays do. In Mark's gospel we don't even see the risen Jesus, just an empty tomb, and the story ends not with joy but on a note of fear (16:8). Stranger still are the accounts of actually encountering the risen Jesus in the other three gospels and the apparent difficulty those gospel writers had in describing those encounters.

While the resurrection accounts in Matthew, Luke, and John share virtually no details in common (which is itself rather curious), all three agree on this much: Encountering the risen Jesus is profoundly disorienting as he is neither a ghost nor a resuscitated corpse. Beyond saying what he is not, however, their language falters. Consider, for example, that none of his closest friends even recognize him when they first encounter him (Luke 24:16; John 20:14). Or consider his apparently incorporeal ability to appear at will behind locked doors and vanish just as quickly while at the same time inviting his friends to touch him (Matthew 28:9; John 20:27), breathing on them (John 20:22), and making a fire on a beach to cook breakfast (John 21:9). In these accounts, the risen Jesus comes across as both mysteriously extraordinary and concretely ordinary at the same time. The gospel writers either abandoned all hope of consistency in their accounts or they were wrestling as best they could with describing uncharted territory, a reality they could not define but only point to and evoke. It was not enough to say that they were simply willing to pick up where Jesus left off before his tragic and untimely death. If that was all these writers wished to say about resurrection, as Rowan Williams has noted, we would be hard-pressed "to account for that echo of bewilderment, shock and disorientation" we find in those stories.[2]

Common threads do emerge in these accounts when we realize that the risen Jesus doesn't cease to be human; in fact, his risen humanity continues to include the physical attributes of a particular body. At the same time, this isn't the kind of human existence with which any of us is yet familiar. Here the gospel writers struggle with how to speak of the risen Jesus just as much as they struggled with speaking about the ministry of Jesus. In both cases, Jesus disrupts cultural assumptions and disturbs expected patterns. These disruptions are not an escape from the particular and often harsh realities of human life and culture. Rather, Jesus points to a different kind of engagement with those realities, toward a more genuinely authentic human existence of which we have received only a glimpse.

Hearing the good news of Jesus as hope for incarnate, fully embodied human thriving shapes Christian faith and ministry in some profound ways. Bodies matter. Not just bodies generally, but particular bodies in particular contexts facing particular hopes and dreams matter. Bodily relationships matter—economic relationships that keep food on my table every day while millions go hungry; ecological relationships that exploit natural resources for the benefit of wealthy nations; sexual relationships that abuse the weak and the vulnerable; and the many relationships in which food is shared and environments are protected and loving families are nurtured. All of these embodied manifestations of human life matter in the most theologically and spiritually profound way. This incarnational insight deepens even further by claiming that the journey toward the fullness of human life continues beyond the grave. That's the startling and disorienting insight those gospel writers tried to capture. As Williams puts it, Jesus does rise but "without simply sloughing off the human condition."[3]

No wonder dancing with this particular Jesus so often feels strange and exotic. No wonder Christian faith can feel alien and unfamiliar, like the hula and hoop dancers did to me. If the good news of the Gospel offers the hope of dancing with God, the steps Jesus offers for the dance are more, not less human than we usually realize, which makes our own particularities not less but more relevant for putting that hope into practice. Speaking about this kind of Christian faith means finding ways to speak about a fully human life in God rather than ignoring or discarding the particularities of human existence. And for us, no less than it did for Jesus, this lifelong process continues even beyond death.

Translating these gospel insights into particular twenty-first-century contexts takes some hard work and discipline. That kind of work started almost immediately, in the very first Christian communities, and has continued for centuries. The challenge in this work is to take the particular first-century Jesus and make him "portable."

THE PORTABLE JESUS

It's one thing for a white Midwesterner like me to hear hula music or the drums of a hoop dance. It's quite another to learn how to dance to those rhythms. Experimenting with new steps involves a host of cultural and historical factors, which one trip to Hawaii or to a Native American dance performance cannot adequately address. Similar complexities occur in hearing the particular music of the gospels and learning how to dance to it in a setting far removed from the one in which the music was first played. How does the particular Jesus of first-century Jerusalem remain relevant in third-century Rome? How do we dance to ancient Middle Eastern rhythms in modern Western societies? Can the particular Jesus become portable?

Americans pose similar questions about our particular form of government. What relevance do the eighteenth-century words of Thomas Jefferson and James Madison hold for twenty-first-century American social policy? Each generation faces the task of translating those early insights into a new context and addressing particular issues the drafters of the U.S. Constitution could not have anticipated. Exporting American democratic insights into other nations and cultures becomes even more perplexing, as every American president quickly discovers. Finding language and strategies appropriate to new circumstances while retaining the insights of previous generations proves no less challenging for Christian theology than it does for American democracy.

The Apostle Paul's letters to various Christian communities offer one of the first examples of trying to make the particular Jesus portable in new contexts. For the most part, those early communities to which Paul wrote faced a variety of cultural issues Jesus had not addressed. Apparently, and to make his task even more daunting, Paul himself didn't experience the ministry of Jesus before the crucifixion. Based on the insights from his own religious tradition as a Jew, building on what he learned from his own encounter with the risen Jesus, and reflecting on the experiences of the communities he founded, Paul created theological language appropriate to particular contexts as far flung from Jerusalem as Rome, Corinth, Ephesus, and Philippi.

The work of creating appropriate theological language, illustrated in both the gospel texts and in Paul's letters, continued in the following centuries. As Christianity spread throughout the Roman Empire, Christian writers and thinkers borrowed the images, symbols, and concepts they believed were the most appropriate to their own contexts for articulating the good news of God-in-Christ, for making the particular first-century insights of Jesus more portable. These various attempts to speak about Jesus sometimes overlapped and, at other times, diverged significantly. Imagine reading two histories about the American continent, one from the perspective of a New England Puritan, the other from a West Coast Spanish conquistador. Or imagine the differences between an Irish Catholic and an English Protestant telling the story of Great Britain as the "United Kingdom." Both accounts would surely have similarities as well as noticeable differences in perspective, emphasis, strategy, and purpose. The same thing is true in the development of Christology, the art and discipline of reflecting on the Jesus of the gospels as the Christ of faith.

Christology developed in much the same way Trinitarian reflection did, as a response to persistent questions about the relationship between Jesus and God. Previous ways of speaking about Divine Reality were no longer adequate based on the experiences and the accounts of encountering Jesus. These early centuries in Christian thought produced a range of options with which those Christians experimented to address such questions, many of which were eventually labeled "heresies," or deviations from the norm Christian communities hoped to establish. Fourth-century followers of a theologian by the name of Arius, for example, rejected the Trinitarian notion of Jesus as the human embodiment of the second "person" of the Trinity, preferring instead to think of God bestowing on Jesus the dignity of "sonship." Followers of Apollinarius, on the other hand, were inclined to think of the human body of Jesus as something like the shell of an egg, which contained not a human spirit but the divine Spirit. Each of these views finds at least some traces of biblical support, depending on which gospel one turns to for help. Combining the insights of all four gospels, on the other hand, proves exceedingly difficult.

Historical theologians often group these early christological options into two broad schools of thought, the Alexandrian and the Antiochene, named after the cities where these ideas flourished. Generally speaking, Alexandrians tended to stress the divinity of Jesus, often at the expense of his full humanity, whereas Antiochenes preferred to stress his humanity, which was later assumed into Divine Reality. This diversity of opinion may have flourished more explicitly and for much longer if the Emperor Constantine had not converted to Christianity in the fourth century.

While Constantine's motives and religious inclinations remain subject to ongoing debate, he certainly worried about the political stability of his vast empire. Like many political leaders before him and to this day, Constantine recognized the potential in religious uniformity as a tool for maintaining social and political control. Granting the church official institutional status in the empire was not quite enough. From Constantine's perspective, the church's internal disagreements required definitive resolution, at least in public. For Constantine, the content of Christian theology itself probably mattered less than reaching consensus about it, for the sake of the empire if not the church.

Constantine eventually convened a council in the city of Nicaea in the year 325, to which he invited some of the more prominent Christian leaders in the empire to resolve lingering and often highly charged questions about Jesus. The Nicene Creed, which most Anglican Christians still recite on Sunday mornings, emerged from that council and became the standard by which to judge theologically appropriate speech: Jesus is both fully human and fully divine. More than that, the structure of the creed itself reflects the evolution of Trinitarian thinking as it firmly unites the "Father" and the "Son" and the "Holy Spirit" in a single Divine Reality. In this way, the Nicene Creed became one of the first ways to make the particular Jesus explicitly portable from one cultural context to the next. The creed became, as it were, the container in which we can carry Jesus with us.

Whether Constantine realized it or not, however, participants in the Council of Nicaea managed to dodge some of the more vexing questions their faith continued to pose. The council never articulated, for example, the precise mechanism by which the second "person" of the Trinity became human, only that the Incarnation was accomplished by the Holy Spirit. Both Alexandrians and Antiochenes could live with that assertion equally well and still maintain their own unique perspectives. Likewise, while the council declared that the Incarnation occurred "for our salvation," they neglected (perhaps intentionally and even wisely) to define exactly from what and for what humans are "saved." To be sure, the council's creed did manage to exclude quite a few possibilities for theologically appropriate speech, but they left room for many more than they themselves may have intended. In this sense, the Nicene Creed is less like a secure container for the portable Jesus and more like a sieve; only the large chunks remain while the many details keep dribbling out. Or, put in another way, while the Nicene Creed establishes our dance floor, it nevertheless offers plenty of room for a variety of steps.

Rowan Williams has wondered whether the traditional assumptions about "orthodoxy" and "heresy" are still useful in this kind of conversation. Today, just as they have in the past, these terms tend to render Christian theology as a series of litmus tests. Orthodox Christians, or "true believers," believe only *this* about Jesus and not *that*. Heretical Christians, on the other hand, refuse to believe what they should. Historically, Williams notes, these terms sometimes functioned in a slightly different way.

The diversity of Trinitarian images in Christian traditions serves as a perpetual reminder that Christians frequently find it easier to identify inadequate language about God than to identify the best language about God. The same is true in the history of speaking about Jesus; the development of Christology exhibits just as much diversity as Trinitarian developments. Christians have thus found it inadequate to speak of Jesus only as a teacher and not also a savior and have likewise found it inadequate to speak of Jesus as divine and not also human. Orthodoxy tries to say more, not less about God than we thought possible, while heresy tries to restrict what we can reasonably say about Divine Reality. "What the early Church condemned as heresy," Williams writes, "was commonly a tidy version of its language, in which the losses were adjudged too severe for comfort . . . in which the losses were adjudged to distort or to limit the range of reference of religious speech."[4] If the dance floor feels cramped, in other words, it's likely heretical, and while the orthodox dance floor does have limits, it likely has more room for a variety of steps than we usually imagine.

Where then do these historical developments take us in our search for a portable Jesus? In many ways, they lead us back to the Apostle Paul, whose first attempts at portability still hold insights today. In retrieving those insights, it's important to remember that Paul probably didn't have the advantage of reading the gospels as we do. Biblical scholars generally date the gospel texts after Paul's first letters. For Paul, this meant preaching the good news and establishing Christian communities without ever having read a gospel! To be sure, he had a dramatic encounter of his own with the risen Jesus and he relied on the stories, instruction, and nurture of the Christians who took him in after that encounter. But that is precisely the point of the theological language Paul created. By finding his life dramatically changed without ever having read a gospel, Paul quickly realized where to find the portable Jesus: in and among Christians themselves.

Prior to his dramatic conversion, Paul (who was then called Saul) had been an ardent and even violent persecutor of Jesus' disciples. According to the book of Acts, while traveling to Damascus with such persecution in mind, he was literally knocked off his feet by a blinding flash of light and a strange voice. "Why are you persecuting me?" the voice asked. "And who are you?" Paul replied. "I am Jesus," the voice said, "whom you are persecuting" (see 9:4–5). Notice that Jesus does not say, "You are persecuting my *followers*." Jesus says, "You are persecuting *me*." We can only imagine the effect this encounter had on Paul; it clearly shaped the innovative theological language he created on the missionary excursions that followed.

Paul's theology has been described in a variety of ways, the emphases of which frequently depend on the particular community to which he was writing and the particular issues those communities faced. Yet at least one thing remains constant in his approach. Paul treated each of the Christian communities to which he wrote as the body of Christ. He did not encourage his readers to think of themselves as somehow like Jesus, or that their various ministries resembled the ministry of Jesus, or that they were continuing in the footsteps of Jesus. Paul was much more explicit than that. "You are the body of Christ," he writes, "and individually members of it" (1 Corinthians 12:27). And this, he goes on to say, is the work of the Holy Spirit.

In John's gospel, the risen Jesus tries to persuade his disciples to think in the same way. As Jesus stands among his disciples, close enough to touch and embrace, he breathes on them and says, "Receive the Holy Spirit. If you forgive the sins of any, they are forgiven them; if you retain the sins of any, they are retained" (20:22–23). Here the disciples are given the very same Spirit that animated Jesus and they are entrusted therefore with the very same ministry Jesus exercised. John, in other words, describes in his gospel what Paul later experienced: The followers of Jesus become the body of Christ.

In ways Christians have found difficult to grasp, let alone to embrace, the particular Jesus, crucified and risen, becomes portable in us through the work of the Holy Spirit. As the body of Christ, the divine music we hear in Jesus also plays in us, inviting us to dance just as Jesus danced. More than this, Jesus encouraged his disciples to broaden the dance and to learn steps he couldn't teach them, steps into which the Spirit would lead them (John 16:13). The choreography Jesus inspires, just as it did in first-century Palestine, doesn't lead us away from but toward the fullness of human life in what the particular Jesus called the kingdom of God. This fullness of life will look slightly different in each new cultural context in which the dance is practiced even though the music is coming from the same source. And just as christological ideas evolve over many centuries, so also our understanding of human thriving continues to grow and change. In this sense, the idea of salvation demands as much portability as Jesus.

THE EUCHARISTIC JESUS

For some of Jesus' disciples, salvation meant overthrowing the Roman Empire and restoring the Davidic kingdom of ancient Israel (Acts 1:6). For some of the Christians in Thessalonica, to whom Paul wrote at least two letters, salvation meant that human beings would no longer die (1 Thessalonians 4:13). Irenaeus, a third-century theologian, imagined salvation as a stealth rescue mission for God's creation, which had been taken captive by Satan. Still others understood salvation as divine forgiveness but offered various views of how that forgiveness is accomplished.

The hope for salvation continues to energize Christian communities even when we're not precisely sure from what and for what we need to be saved. The various approaches to this issue in the Bible and in subsequent centuries of reflection all have at least this much in common: The hope of salvation is a way to speak about the human longing to thrive with abundant life. In John's gospel, Jesus described his ministry with that hope clearly in view, that all might have life "and have it abundantly" (10:10). Rather than just one thing, there are many things that can make us stumble on that journey into human thriving. Human beings appear to share some of those stumbling blocks in common, while others are historically and culturally specific and even unique to particular individuals. Whatever prevents us from thriving, Christian faith offers the hope that God continually invites us into the dance of abundant life and will provide us with the means to dance better after we stumble. Because even more than we do, God longs to see us thrive.

Christians hear this divine invitation to thrive whenever we gather around the eucharistic table to share a simple meal. At that table, the particular Jesus and the portable Jesus come together in the eucharistic Jesus, in the gestures, the postures, the bread and the wine, and the words we prayerfully remember: "This is my body; this is my blood." Performing this act together recalls the many occasions in which the historical Jesus shared meals, including the final meal he shared with his friends on the night he was betrayed. Our common prayer around that table also recalls the many centuries of theological reflection on what this eucharistic meal means, what it can tell us about God-in-Christ, the particular ways it inspires us to live, and how it invites us to see our lives and the world as essentially and fundamentally a gift. That's what the Greek word *eucharist* means—thanksgiving.

Just as there are many types of dancing, there are various ways to describe the hope of salvation inspired by the eucharistic Jesus. As the Book of Common Prayer has evolved in the national provinces of the Anglican Communion, Anglican Christians today pray with various versions of that one book, and each of them contains more than one eucharistic prayer. While each of these prayers follows the same basic pattern and rhythm, the text of each prayer varies in terms of metaphor, symbol, and emphasis. In the American Prayer Book alone the four distinct eucharistic prayers (or six, including the two rendered in more traditional language) offer images of cosmic restoration, atoning sacrifice, rescue from evil, freedom for prisoners, good news for the poor, and the way of peace and reconciliation, to name just a few. In this sense, the development of the Prayer Book mirrors the development of Christian scripture and the development of Christology. Just as there is more than one gospel in the Bible, there is more than one eucharistic prayer in the Prayer Book. The mystery of God-in-Christ cannot be contained in a single biblical text any more than the mystery of salvation can be contained and spoken in a single prayer.

The breadth of reflection on the eucharistic Jesus is often obscured or narrowed by the assumptions ingrained in so many of us, either from the religious education of our childhood or from the images pervading popular culture. This has certainly been the case among the visitors I talk with in my congregation, where we experiment with a variety of liturgical forms and with ways to speak about the good news of God-in-Christ. Regardless of the texts we use or the freshness of the language we offer, visitors (and probably more than a few longtime members) almost always hear what they expect to hear: Jesus died for my sins so I can go to heaven. There are certainly some good reasons for hearing Christian faith in that way, which has been a recurring theme in the way Christian traditions have been presented and disseminated in modern Western societies. That theme is reinforced by the fact that every eucharistic liturgy commemorates the betrayal, suffering, death, and resurrection of Jesus. But that's not the only thing those liturgies commemorate. By restricting the idea and the hope of salvation to the mechanisms of violent sacrifice, we risk missing the rich and deeply textured invitation God extends to us in Christ. We risk missing the invitation to dance if we mistake the music of the Incarnation for a funeral dirge.

The relative freedom from any one doctrinal system in Anglican theologies offers an opportunity to recover a broader view of salvation and the practice of hope such views inspire. By turning to the Incarnation just as frequently as to the crucifixion, Anglican theologies reflect on the purpose of human life and not merely the remedy for its failures. By celebrating the birth in Bethlehem with as much devotion as remembering the death in

Jerusalem, Anglicans avoid reducing Christian faith to a morbid obsession with pain and suffering. This approach does not in any way mitigate the significance of the crucifixion; to the contrary, it actually broadens its significance by detaching it from its typically exclusive link to systems of sacrificial atonement.

Understanding the death of Jesus as an atoning sacrifice for the sake of salvation resonates with some but certainly not all biblical writers. The notion of atonement appears explicitly in the letter to the Hebrews, where the writer turns to images of animal sacrifice in ancient Israelite religion for his reflections. For that writer, those images of sacrifice provide the best way to describe the death of Jesus as atoning, as the mechanism, so to speak, of divine forgiveness.[5] On the other hand, this interpretation of Jesus' death as an atoning sacrifice doesn't fit very well with some of the gospel stories. The gospel writers would seem to question the necessity of crucifixion for forgiveness when they show Jesus forgiving sins *before* his death (Matthew 9:2; Mark 2:10; Luke 7:47).

In addition to a few biblical texts, the concept of salvation with which many Christians live today derives mostly from the twelfth-century theology of Anselm, whose work articulated a particular aspect of Christian thought that had been percolating for some time. Anselm's theory of salvation, usually referred to as "substitutionary atonement," relied heavily on the cultural and political realities of medieval Europe. The configurations of a feudal society, together with the legacy of Roman jurisprudence, rooted Anselm's approach in a particular kind of legal system in which violations of the law demanded appropriate satisfaction. Borrowing from these cultural developments, Anselm understood the death of Jesus as the satisfaction of divine justice. The death of Jesus, in other words, paid the price for our sins, for our violations of divine law, which we ourselves could not pay.

While this Anselmian theme has permeated Western Christian theology— so much so that many Christians today likely adopt some version of it without ever having heard of Anselm—this view by no means represents the full range of reflection on the hope of salvation, either from ancient sources or from Anselm's own contemporaries. Greek or Eastern approaches, for example, which developed apart from the more heavily juridical context of Western Europe, usually place greater emphasis on the Incarnation. Rather than the satisfaction of a debt owed to divine justice, the Incarnation points to a much broader commitment to the project of human thriving. According to these views, the hope of salvation comes from God's own willingness to enter the human dance and lead us into the fullness of human life that God intended from the beginning.

Even in these Eastern theological views, the stress on an incarnational hope does not simply erase human sinfulness. The human condition is still clearly riddled with what Christian traditions call sin, as anyone can see today just by reading a daily newspaper. The worldwide human family struggles every day with any number of roadblocks to human thriving, whether in violent conflict and war, or economic deprivation, or institutional tyranny and oppression. The execution of Jesus, even though he was innocent of both the religious and the political charges brought against him, simply bears witness to the sinful condition from which humanity must be saved. The hope for salvation, however, must surely inspire more than relief from guilt or the forbearance of an otherwise angry God. We are no doubt in desperate need of forgiveness for any number of things, from both God and other human beings, but we clearly need more than that.

The fear human beings harbor over mistakes and shortcomings is surely not the only fear from which we must be saved. The experience of guilt taps into a more fundamental anxiety—the fear that humanity itself is deeply flawed, that just being human is itself a profound "mistake." This, Christian traditions seem to say, is the fear from which each of us needs to be saved. A broader view of salvation inspires us to embrace human existence as fundamentally good and to live with the hope of breaking through the many roadblocks to human thriving so each and every one can dance to the divine music of abundant life.[6]

Anglican theologians encourage this broader view of Christian hope by refusing to choose between the manger and the cross as the primary mechanism of divine salvation. Anglicans do not celebrate Christmas as merely the historical preface to Good Friday. The hope of salvation is too rich and deep to confine it in any one moment of Jesus' life or even in our own lives. Drawing on biblical insights and subsequent theological traditions, Anglican Christianity imagines salvation extending over the whole course of Jesus' life, ministry, teaching, death, and resurrection, and beyond the empty tomb into the energizing presence of the Spirit and in the life and ministry of Christian communities.

In all its many forms, the hope of salvation provides a shorthand way of speaking about the entire story of dancing with God. That story begins with

God's own desire for communion in creation, the divine embrace of Israel as God's own beloved, the extension of that embrace to the whole human family in Jesus, and the hope of living into a genuine and authentic humanity, which Christians put into practice as the body of Christ. This is the far-reaching, wide-embracing story we hear from the eucharistic Jesus every Sunday morning. To reduce this story of salvation to that which is accomplished by the suffering and death of Jesus tragically misses the point; it says far too little about the dance. Or to recall Rowan Williams's insight about "heresy," we should not worry about saying too much but about not saying enough when we speak of salvation.

Meanwhile, the Western juridical model of salvation, epitomized by Anselm, continues to inform the minds and hearts of many Christians today. For some, it's the only salvific music they can hear. This kind of music shapes how people dance with the eucharistic Jesus in some profound ways, mostly by distorting the relationship between salvation and ethics. Narrowing the focus of salvation to the need of forgiveness quickly turns ethics into a system of rules and God looks mostly like a lawmaker.

If, on the other hand, salvation is viewed more broadly, as God's invitation to abundant life and to authentic human thriving, ethics suddenly expands onto a much wider dance floor and takes on a more urgent rhythm. As we gather around the eucharistic table on Sunday morning, we start to fret less about which of the Ten Commandments each of us may have broken during the week and worry more about the welfare mother, one paycheck away from homelessness; or about the potential change in zoning laws that would transform a regional park into a shopping mall; or the number of children who die every day from preventable diseases; or the disparity between corporate salaries and the wages we pay the teachers of our children; or the resources Western nations spend on their militaries compared to the money spent on global hunger.

Refocusing ethics toward these cultural and political concerns does not mean abandoning any reflection on the Ten Commandments. It does mean recognizing the social ramifications of our life choices rather than obsessing over our individual faults and shortcomings. It does mean adjusting our concept of Divine Reality from that of rule maker to choreographer, one who yearns to see everyone join in the dance of abundant life. Rather than approaching ethics as a series of hoops to jump through, God-in-Christ invites us to pick up those hoops and dance with them. Holy hoop dancing doesn't make Christian ethics any easier; it actually becomes more difficult, as it requires the practiced agility and focused bodily attention of a hula dancer.

Understanding Christian ethics as primarily a communal endeavor deepens our life with God well beyond the level of individual scrupulosity. Learning to dance to the music of Jesus means sorting through, analyzing, and evaluating the interweaving layers of politics, social policy, economic systems, and cultural paradigms, and all for the sake of both discerning and embracing the kind of genuinely authentic human life God intends. This is precisely the point made by John L. Kater Jr., an Episcopal priest and moral theologian, reflecting on his experiences in Latin America, especially concerning the economic relationships between the Northern and Southern Hemispheres. "The healing of the world," Kater writes, "requires more than individual conversion. This task gives ample opportunity for us all—individuals and congregations alike—to act on behalf of the fullness of life God wills for us. Some of our actions will be directed to immediate or short-term solutions, but we must never allow ourselves to forget that in the end it is the fundamental structures of our life together that must be rebuilt."[7]

Hearing the eucharistic Jesus invite us to dance, God's own passion for life seizes our imaginations, compelling us to work more intentionally for that abundant life God intends for all. This is the work of salvation, the great incarnate dance of life into which God-in-Christ invites us. William Temple pointedly described this incarnational approach to Christian faith by noting that Christianity "is the most materialistic of the world's religions."[8] With this comment, Temple wished to stretch our imaginations to see the far-reaching implications of the Incarnation for every aspect of our lives, personally, socially, and ecologically.

The diversity of approaches to Christology in the Bible and the many ways Christian communities have tried to speak about the Incarnation caution against trying to find just one formula or image for the good news of God-in-Christ. Embracing multiple views and listening to various perspectives can fuel faithful imaginations as we try to discern how God is inviting us to dance. Anglican Christians do this kind of theological work by sustaining genuine conversation and fostering ongoing conversion whenever we gather to share a simple meal of bread and wine. Taking Temple's comment to heart in those eucharistic moments invites us to imagine an intimate union between Earth and heaven, between spirit and flesh, between human and divine. Only faithful imaginations will suffice for putting that kind of hope into practice in the many material ways human beings culturally, politically, and economically interact with each other.

In short, God's great dance of life does not lead us off the stage of this earthly dance floor. To the contrary, the eucharistic Jesus—in all his wild, undomesticated, and earthly rhythms—invites each of us to dance with our feet firmly planted on the particular and concrete dance floors of human life and culture. This is the truly exotic dance of the body of Christ, and its peculiar steps will vary depending on the particular cultural contexts in which the hope of that dance is practiced. As the Apostle Paul noted so long ago, learning those steps leads us rather quickly into that mysterious and seductive energy Christian traditions have called the Holy Spirit.

5

THE TANGO
~ A Spirituality of Divine Seduction ~

Some of the assumptions I used to harbor about various types of dancing taught me something about similar assumptions I had made concerning Christian faith and theology. By taking lessons in both jazz and country-and-western line dancing, for example, I came to appreciate the motor skills and hard work required for dancing well to those kinds of steps. Other types of dancing, like ballroom-style waltzes, seemed far less rigorous and, I assumed, did not require the same kind of athleticism. The fluid grace of a waltz simply looked calming and relaxing and certainly nothing that would cause one to breathe heavily or break a sweat.

A Trinitarian Christian faith can carry similar assumptions, as it did for me, about the three divine "persons" of the Trinity. Both the ongoing work of the Divine Composer and the rigorous steps of the Incarnate Dancer suggest the kind of practiced skill and disciplined performance of well-rehearsed choreography. The "third" in Divine Reality, on the other hand, what Christian traditions have called the "Holy Spirit," shows up on the theological scene with far less precision, looking a bit soft around the edges and rather vague. The religious tradition of my childhood paid relatively little attention to this divine Third apart from occasional references to the "Comforter" Jesus promised to send (John 15:26). That kind of language evoked for me an image of my mother tucking me into a warm bed on a cold, rainy night—an image of Divine Reality I still cherish. But that image

111

also perpetuates some particular theological assumptions: Jesus does the hard work of choreography while the Holy Spirit makes the dance fluid and comfy. I began to reevaluate the sufficiency of that image after attending my first ballroom dancing competition, during which I discovered just how wrong my assumptions had been about that particular style of dance.

Early on in the competition, I realized that even the dancers who stood virtually no chance of winning outpaced my basic skills by far. Not only did those couples know the fluid steps of the dance; they could do them while moving quickly and gracefully around the entire dance floor without intruding into another couple's space. This required as much skill as learning the intricate steps themselves. The dancers had to pay attention not only to their partners but also to the other couples and to the ever-changing landscape of the dance floor. All the couples managed to do this without any independent direction from coaches or friends on the "sidelines." Imagine an airport without an air traffic control tower. Would you entrust the responsibility for avoiding collisions to the pilots?

To be sure, each ballroom competition has its fair share of near misses on the dance floor. A couple sometimes find themselves boxed into a corner or heading into a logjam of bodies. This happens more frequently than I can usually discern, since the most highly skilled dancers are able to dance themselves out of those near misses without missing a beat. Avoiding collisions seemed especially remarkable to me when watching a tango, which can take dramatic and sudden turns on the dance floor. Observing those couples paying attention to the other dancers and navigating the space while at the same time maintaining the tango's energy with their partners frequently took my breath away. Unless you have actually witnessed it, the energy, the skill, and the electric bond between the dancers proves quite difficult to describe.

The tango is arguably the quintessential dance of seduction and romance. This may be especially true for North Americans, who tend to associate the rhythms of Latin music with the sultry and enticing humidity of the tropics. Still, the postures of the couple's bodies, the occasional and sudden gaze they fix on each other, and the lines they trace across the floor all generate an undeniably erotic energy, and not only between the dancers but also for those who watch and find themselves lured into the tango's pulsating rhythms.

After observing several couples move through the narrative arc of the tango, I began to notice something a bit curious. Even with the tango's clearly defined roles of leader and follower—a key feature in any ballroom-style dancing—it was by no means clear who was seducing whom. Some probably assume the man, as the "leader," is leading the woman into the adventure of romantic love. Depending on cultural perspectives, others might assume the woman, supposedly the follower, is the one who seduces. As I reflected on this, I actually began to wonder whether I was the one being seduced by the couple's energy as it was welling up and spilling off the dance floor.

The tango itself never quite resolves the dynamic between leading and following, which makes its energy even more enticing. I noticed this particular feature of the dance on a more practical level as well, when a couple managed to avoid colliding with other dancers only because the "follower" gently nudged the "leader" back into some open space. That was the moment when watching a dance competition suddenly turned into a moment of theological insight. As each couple found the breathing space they needed for expressing the energy between them, I understood Christian spirituality in a new way, especially its more dynamic and even seductive and erotic qualities.

The word "spirituality" now functions as a remarkably wide umbrella term to describe a host of disciplines and practices. Disillusionment with religious institutions has led many in contemporary Western societies to abandon traditional religious formation and experiment with a variety of spiritualities, frequently with no reference to any particular religious tradition or school of thought. For others, spirituality refers to regular participation in the rhythm of the church's sacramental life, digesting as best they can the various doctrines articulated in Christian theology. In either case, the most obvious aspect of the word spirituality itself is strangely absent: the Spirit.

Neglecting any explicit mention of the Spirit in spiritual practices reflects a long history of not knowing quite what to make of this concept. Especially today, in an age of science and technology, we are naturally skeptical of trying to speak of the intangible and immaterial rather than of the concrete and particular things we know how to identify, analyze, dissect, manipulate, and control. Human language never quite manages to capture the ephemeral, uncanny, or inscrutable. We can, for example, talk about the steps one must learn for the tango, the kind of music to which such steps respond, and the positions and gestures of the bodies dancing to that kind of music. Apart from those concrete and particular things, it becomes quite difficult to know how to speak about the fluid motion of the dance itself, or the enticingly erotic energy it creates between the dancers, or how it feels to watch the dance unfold. These are the intangible qualities we want mostly to talk about when speaking of the tango, yet they continually elude precision in our speech, like water slipping through the fingers of cupped hands. The same difficulties appear in trying to speak about the Spirit.

The history of English-speaking Christianity adds another layer of difficult in speaking about spirituality. Both Christians and non-Christians likely associate the Spirit with the more traditional language of the "Holy Ghost." That kind of language can lead quite naturally to assuming that the Spirit refers to the ghost of the risen Jesus. Or, as a friend of mine likes to say, it sounds like we're talking about a divine poltergeist clanging about in our cathedral belfries.

In modern English translations of the Bible, the words rendered as "spirit" have nothing at all to do with ghosts. Even "spirit" doesn't quite suffice. In Hebrew the word is *ruach*; in Greek it's *pneuma*. In both cases, a better translation would be either "breath" or "wind." Even the Latin verb *spirare*, from which we derive the word "spirit," means "to breathe." Anyone who has suffered from pneumonia will have no trouble remembering these ancient words. The name for that particular lung ailment comes from the Greek word for breath. Knowing even this much about Greek can add a bit more texture to the otherwise slippery qualities of the word spirituality. John's gospel points in that direction by making puns.

In the third chapter of John, Jesus tries to explain the dynamics of religious faith to a religious leader by the name of Nicodemus. To see the kingdom of God, Jesus says, you must be born of the Spirit (*pneuma*). As Nicodemus finds this perplexing, Jesus explains further: "The wind (*pneuma*) blows where it chooses . . . you do not know where it comes from or where it goes. So it is with everyone who is born of the Spirit (*pneuma*)" (John 3:8). Religious faith, in other words, involves a dramatic change of life, like being born all over again. It's like the wind, Jesus says, rising up when we least expect it and blowing away the past, like so many layers of dust in the attic before a newly opened window on a breezy day. When John returns to the same pun in the accounts of the resurrection, the imagery shifts toward the intimate and the practical. As the risen Jesus stands among his disciples, he breathes on them and says, "Receive holy breath (*pneuma*)," the same word he used with Nicodemus in talking about the wind. The result in this case, however, is the practice of forgiveness (20:22–23).

Anglican Christians generally approach the Spirit with the more practical if not pragmatic sensibilities associated with the work of forgiveness and reconciliation. Convinced of the essential link between theology and ethics, or thought and action, Anglicans understand spirituality as the ongoing attempt to shape our day-to-day conduct of life according to the insights we discern from Christian traditions. If the eucharistic Jesus invites us to dance, he does so not only in church but also in economic and political choices, in places of work, in families, in play and recreation, and wherever the Spirit happens to lead. In this sense, spirituality is the way to talk about the link between reflecting on the choreography and actually learning the dance steps on the dance floor. It likewise refers to the process of taking lessons from the dance floor back into our reflection on the choreography itself.

Practical, nuts-and-bolts approaches to spirituality resonate well with particular European and especially North American sensibilities. Americans like to get things done and, if at all possible, in an orderly fashion. At the same time, a practical construe of spirituality doesn't quite blend in very well with the dramatic irruptions attributed to the Spirit throughout Christian history: in the Great Awakening in colonial New England; in the lives of medieval mystics caught up in moments of ecstasy; or among biblical writers, who describe dancing tongues of flame (Acts 2:3) and being carried away into visions of the "third heaven," whatever that might mean (2 Corinthians 12:2). At the very least, the exuberance of life in the Spirit observed in Pentecostal congregations seems quite different from typically Anglican approaches to spirituality. It's one thing to dance gracefully to a waltz and quite another to be swept away by the energy of a tango.

Anglican Christianity, no less than any other mainstream Christian denomination, has had trouble knowing precisely what to "do" with the Spirit. This ambivalence derives in part from the more general tendency of Western Christian theologies to focus almost exclusively on Jesus, on questions of Christology. This tendency simply mirrors the pattern of the Christian scriptures, which deal mostly with the meaning and significance of Jesus. That pattern is later intensified by the bond Western traditions forged between the crucifixion and the idea of salvation as forgiveness. In such a pattern, the Spirit might as well be a jigsaw puzzle piece left over after the picture has already been assembled.

On the other hand, Anglican communities exhibit a perpetual tension between traditional insights and innovative practices, a tension Anglican theologies never quite resolve in any neat or tidy way. In a variety of ways, Anglicans continually entertain the possibility of modifying language about Divine Reality based on the lessons learned from our attempts to dance. This "breathing space" in theological traditions makes room for the kind of course correction any religious community needs to make on the dance floor: It keeps our dancing lively and fresh. We can quite properly attribute such breathing space to what Christian traditions have called the Holy Spirit. Describing that breathing space adequately, however, has not been easy.

Retrieving insights about the Spirit from historical traditions turns out to be even more challenging than finding appropriate words and images for Jesus. Jesus of Nazareth inspires much more concrete and manageable ways of talking and speaking and acting than the unseen energies of the Spirit. Talking about the Spirit means giving voice to something as close to us as our own breath and as illusive as the wind. While the typically Anglican reliance on the practice of hope offers help for talking about the Spirit, it will not necessarily lead to tidy theological models. As Christian communities often discover, encountering the divine energy of the Spirit doesn't necessarily feel comfortable and cozy, at least not at first. This energy quite frequently makes Christians restless, eager to find better ways to speak about Divine Reality and continually to reevaluate the dynamics of our common life. This is the restlessness of hope itself, reluctant to settle down in theological systems, impatient with intractable institutional structures, and driven forward by seemingly impossible visions of human thriving.

Practicing a Spirit-driven hope will resemble the energy of a tango, which is both unexpectedly dramatic and breathtakingly intimate. It will rely on recognizing the Spirit in ever new and expanding ways, sometimes like the interruptions of a strong wind and at others, like the enticing whispers of a soft breeze moving over our skin. Over time, it will slowly blur the traditional distinctions between leading and following in our dance with God. We will instead find ourselves happily seduced by the dance itself, and maybe even a bit surprised by how grateful we are for the diversity of the dancers.

THE DIVINE WIND

For some people, falling in love strikes quite suddenly and unexpectedly. For others, it blossoms slowly, over time. In either case, it disrupts the pattern of otherwise ordinary routines. We relish these romantic interludes as refreshing and pleasing if not exhilarating interruptions of usual expectations. The fluid and yet quite distinct and often dramatic turns and shifts of a tango clearly bear witness to the disruptive seduction of romance, as unpredictable as the wind.

The first chapter of Genesis begins with a mighty wind from God sweeping over the waters, bringing creation from the chaos (1:2), the same wind, presumably, that parted the waters of the Red Sea as the Israelites fled Egypt (Exodus 14:21) and that rattled a valley of dry bones into a living, breathing community (Ezekiel 37:9). Each of these references to divine wind can just as easily translate as "spirit," which, no less than romantic seduction, disrupts ordinary and routine rhythms. This is the same spirit-wind that came upon Mary of Nazareth as she found herself surprisingly pregnant (Luke 1:35); that drove her son into the desert before his ministry (Mark 1:12); that gave his disciples the ability to speak in languages they had never studied (Acts 2:4); that transported Philip into a surprising encounter with an Ethiopian eunuch (Acts 8:29); that pushed Peter to embrace Gentiles as worthy as anyone else to find their lives blown over by this divine wind (Acts 11:12); and that gave to one called John a vision of heavenly worship (Revelation 4:2).

Needless to say, these seductive disruptions of ordinary life don't fit very comfortably into the orderly mechanisms of an institution, the functioning of which often depends on a well-oiled bureaucratic adherence to policies and procedures. As early Christian communities grew and evolved toward a structured religious institution, the uncanny energy of life in the Spirit required a bit more organizational intent. This was clearly the case after the fourth-century conversion of Constantine, when the church was suddenly endorsed by the state, but hints of it appear in the varying approaches biblical writers took to questions of communal structure. Stories from the Acts of the Apostles, for example, describe the charismatic endowments of early Christian leaders, which Paul later identifies as particular gifts of the Spirit, whether for teaching, serving, preaching, or healing. Before long, descriptions of Christian leadership rely less on the unpredictable divine "charismata" (spiritual gifts) and more on meeting the requisite qualifications of predetermined roles and offices (1 Timothy 3:1, 8–12).

After Constantine's conversion, the task of defining the parameters of proper Christian speech took some decisive turns, and with it, the structure of both Christian theology and the church as an institution appeared in sharper outline. There's no reason to suppose this kind of development would be any different from similar experiences with all sorts of human organizations. Garden clubs eventually elect a recording secretary. Softball teams eventually need an equipment manager. Even housekeeping tasks benefit from finding a place for everything and keeping everything in its proper place (which I greatly admire, if only as an aspiration). So also with the ancient household called church, where theological housekeepers created clearly defined roles for the family members and found a proper place for each of the household goods, the doctrines of Christian faith.

Finding a proper place for the Spirit, however, continually eluded their grasp, like wondering which guestroom to use for an idiosyncratic cousin visiting for the holidays. Eventually, these householders put their Trinitarian impulses to work in the traditional pattern outlined in the Nicene Creed: God the "Father" is especially associated with the work of creation; God the "Son" is especially associated with salvation; and God the "Holy Spirit," while acknowledged as the voice of the prophets, is associated especially with the church and the church's sacramental life. I must admit to finding such orderly schemas profoundly satisfying, in much the same way I relish color-coded labels for my file folders and arranging freshly laundered socks in my dresser drawer. Still, in Christian theology, that kind of satisfaction comes with significant risk, as anyone quickly discovers when trying to contain the wind.

The impulse to categorize Divine Reality neatly and precisely springs equally from the need to exercise control, often for the sake of maintaining a position of institutional power, as well as from the desire to make Christian faith intelligible and sensible. Responding to that dual impulse, theologians will sometimes try to construct a well-ordered narrative from the texts of the Bible as a way to support the systematic links among various doctrines. The theological work of a twelfth-century monk by the name of Joachim offers a classic case in point.

In trying to describe a visionary insight about the Holy Trinity, Joachim referred to the Hebrew scriptures, especially those dealing with the era of Israel's patriarchs, as the "Age of the Father," which overlaps with the era recorded in the Gospels and in the earliest centuries of Christian thought as the "Age of the Son," which in turn overlaps (not so surprisingly) with Joachim's own era as the "Age of the Spirit." Relatively few Christians today have ever heard of Joachim, even though his schematic approach to the

Trinity and human history continues to shape the assumptions about the Bible and Christian theology still prevalent in many of today's churches. Generally speaking, these assumptions thrive on finding a single narrative thread in the Bible, or trying to speak about "the biblical story." Telling that story usually begins with God the Creator, who is quite properly an angry judge of the stubborn Israelites, and who prepares the way for Jesus, or God the Savior, who atones for our sins on the cross, which then makes room for God the Holy Spirit, who creates the "real" Israel called the Church.

I grew up with that kind of construction of the biblical story, which informed my understanding of Christian faith for many years. But such a tidy biblical chronology bears virtually no resemblance to what the Bible actually says. The texts of the Bible, though neatly contained between two covers of a single book, resist any reduction to a single plot or narrative structure. Those texts certainly don't support the common tendency to think of the Holy Spirit as a latecomer to the divine dance, someone who shows up only after the resurrection of Jesus. Even a brief overview of biblical texts reveals quite a range of diverse narratives and types of literature in which the Spirit plays an active role: a creation narrative (Genesis 1–2); a practical wisdom narrative (the story of Joseph, for example, in Genesis 41); a liberation narrative (the exodus from Egypt); a political narrative (the anointing of kings); a mystical narrative (as in Ezekiel or Daniel); a social justice narrative (the Hebrew prophets); a messianic narrative (the Gospels); a community-building narrative (Acts of the Apostles and Paul's letters); and an apocalyptic narrative (the Revelation to John).

Far from reducing to a single plot or narrative structure, the texts of the Bible continually frustrate attempts to construct just one. The biblical stories themselves identify this disruption of tidy plots as the work of the Spirit. Biblical theologian Hans Frei described this kind of Spirit work by noting how modern biblical interpreters have been so hot in pursuit of the truth of a biblical passage that "texts were often left little breathing space."[1] A good interpretation of a text, Frei went on to suggest, is one in which there is always something left unresolved about the text, something left to bother us and to keep us asking questions. This is the divinely disruptive work of the Spirit who comes unexpectedly to interrupt the construction of tidy and often restrictive systems of thought with fresh and at a times unsettling breezes. When trying to identify who and what the Spirit is in biblical texts, we will find ourselves relying less on systematic patterns and more on novelty:

less on logical analysis and deduction and more on parable and metaphor; less on predictable narrative arcs and more on sudden plot twists and surprises. Nearly every account of encountering the Spirit, both in the Bible and in subsequent Christian history, tends to evoke rather than explain, invite rather than prove, and rather than regulating or circumscribing, the Spirit in these accounts unlocks, unfurls, and propels the humans caught up in that divine wind toward a horizon they had not previously imagined.

Jesus referred to this divine wind as the "Comforter," which would surely urge a revision of what we usually mean by "comfort." Actually, that Greek word in John's gospel translates better as either "advocate" or "helper." Even so, what kind of help do we suppose this divine wind will provide when it puts old patterns of relationship at risk, threatens to turn worldviews upside down, and makes us vulnerable to life-changing encounters? Carefully planned spiritual disciplines and neatly arranged doctrinal systems are quite beside the point as the Spirit breaks out of each and every category the human mind creates for it and shatters each and every organization that seeks to control it. The Spirit does not appear on command but blows where it wills, like the wind. It embarrasses religious leaders by showing up where it's not supposed to (Numbers 11:26–30), blessing people who supposedly don't deserve it (Acts 15:6–11), animating communities the rest of us would prefer to forget (Mark 9:38–41), creating friends from fearful enemies (Acts 9:26–27), and generally stirring up the pot when the cooks thought the stew was already finished.

According to both biblical stories and accounts from later Christian communities, the "help" fallible and shortsighted human beings usually need appears first as profound disorientation and a scrambling of expectations. I think of this kind of help living in the San Francisco Bay Area as bay breezes blow away our seasonal morning fog. As the fog bank lifts and I can see the wide and expansive horizon of the Pacific Ocean beyond the Golden Gate Bridge, the parameters within which I thought I was living suddenly seem small and restricted. In the same way, just when the tango-dancing couple seems sure to find themselves boxed into a corner, the dance takes a dramatic turn into much needed breathing space. Thankfully, the Spirit wind does not always resemble a gale. As the horizons expand and the open spaces appear, the mighty wind from God can soften. As we catch our breath in that newly opened space, we discover an equally breathtaking intimacy.

THE DIVINE BREATH

Few people today lend much credence to greeting card sentiments. "Love means never having to say you're sorry," for example, is a good recipe for a failed relationship. Love means precisely the opposite—a deeper commitment to seeking forgiveness and reconciliation than we adopt among casual acquaintances. At the same time, the intimacy born from romantic love can make the work of forgiveness a bit easier. Erotic energy tends to dissipate both anger and resentment a bit more quickly than the energy among colleagues or neighbors or even siblings. It's at least difficult if not impossible to find oneself simultaneously in the throes of passionate desire for the beloved and furiously demanding an apology. The sharp edges of the offending moment are quickly blunted by the desire itself. And as people in love often admit, the intimacy created by erotic energy can't be summoned on command. It has a life of its own, quite independent of the lovers drawn together by its energy. We can speak in similar ways about the kind of spirituality Christian faith invites us to practice in our relationships as the body of Christ.

Moments of conversion, for individuals and institutions, often transpire when we least expect them. Like the wind, they rise up unbidden, as if from nowhere. By the same token, we cannot coerce or engineer moments of genuine forgiveness and reconciliation. These are the fruits of carefully tended intimacy. Apart from such intimate relations, forgiveness can resemble something more like a negotiated truce, liable at any moment to fall back into hostility or enmity.

Christian spirituality thrives equally on moments of conversion, as dramatic as a sudden wind, and far more subtle moments of intimacy, like a soft breath against your cheek. It resembles the tango, which takes sudden course changes on the dance floor while still nurturing the closeness of a whispered breath. Both of these elements play important roles in John's gospel as Jesus explains to Nicodemus how the Spirit blows where it wills, like the wind, and later stands among his disciples, breathing on them. This latter image suggests a moment of remarkable intimacy, which we can begin to grasp by realizing the physical proximity required actually to breathe on someone. To do so, one needs to be at least close enough to hear the person whisper.

In this encounter with the risen Jesus, the disciples had met together with fear and deep regret. What had happened to Jesus on the cross, they realized, could just as easily happen to them. What's more, the depth of their own betrayal and abandonment of Jesus, whom they loved, pierced them with inconsolable grief. It was then, according to John's gospel, that Jesus appeared among them, close enough for them to see the scars of his cruci-fied body. Even more, he was close enough to breathe on them, which is pre-cisely what he did, saying, "receive holy breath" (20:22).

The intimacy of this encounter mutes any questions the disciples may have harbored about their own forgiveness. Jesus does not need to say, "I for-give you"; the proximity of his breath says enough. This intimacy did not, however, say enough about forgiving each other. In their betrayal of Jesus they had likewise betrayed the love that had made them a community. "Receive holy breath," Jesus says, and then quickly adds, while I imagine looking rather pointedly at each of them, "if you forgive the sins of any, they are forgiven them; if you retain the sins of any, they are retained" (20:23). With these words, Jesus invites them to see the intimacy each of them shares with him as an intimacy they share with each other. And the breath he imparts to each is the breath they exchange among themselves: "If you for-give the sins of any, they are forgiven them."

Identifying the breath in this encounter as the Holy Spirit—which English translations of the Bible encourage—reorients some persistent theo-logical assumptions. The offer of divine forgiveness, for example, issues not from the dying Jesus on the cross, but from the Spirit imparted by the risen Jesus. This is the same Spirit animating the ministry of Jesus before his death, breaking down cultural and religious barriers to communion in the scandal of shared meals with outcasts; expanding notions of kinship well beyond the strictly traced ties of biological origin; luring and enticing both foe and stranger into ever-closer circles of intimacy. In the chaos of betrayal, abandonment, suffering, and death, this same Spirit recreates the intimate dance of communion, not by erasing the chaos—the marks of crucifixion are still visible on Jesus' hands and feet—but by shaping the choreography with forgiveness. This is the same Spirit hovering over the waters of formless chaos in Genesis, giving voice to the deep desire for communion in the act of creation, and refusing to allow even death to thwart that desire.

The desire for communion and the energy of the desire infuses every-thing else Christians have tried and keep trying to say about Divine Reality and about our own longing for intimacy, no matter how haltingly expressed or poorly articulated. The failure to put this desire into satisfying practice only intensifies the longing. Indeed, the need for forgiveness and reconciliation would quickly lose its potency apart from the desire for intimate communion from which the need for forgiveness springs. Stumbling on the dance floor would matter far less if we didn't care so much about the dance itself. Likewise, for the sake of the dance, we pick ourselves up and start dancing again even if we're unsure whether we'll dance any more gracefully than we did before; the energy of the dance simply compels us. As Rowan Williams describes it, forgiveness does not merely look backward, referring only to a misdeed of the past. Forgiveness itself inspires a different vision for the future. "Forgiveness," Williams writes, "is precisely the deep and abiding sense of what relation—with God or with other human beings—can and should be; and so it is itself a stimulus, an irritant, necessarily provoking protest at impoverished versions of social and personal relations."[2]

Each of these elements of the dance—the desire to dance, the energy of the dance, and the grace to dance again when we stumble—is a way to speak about the Holy Spirit, the Divine Breath Jesus breathes on fearful, guilt-ridden disciples. These interrelated elements also provide a way to speak about Christian spirituality, a life that will exhibit the same kind of passion for reconciliation born from erotic energy.

Many Christians are understandably apprehensive about using the language of erotic desire to speak about Christian spirituality. Contemporary Western societies seem simultaneously obsessed with human sexuality and profoundly conflicted over its explicit expression. The many distortions of human sexual relations with which we live today—from domestic violence and abuse to a thriving international slave trade of sex workers and high-profile cases of date rape and incest—all conspire to sever the links between particularly incarnate, sexual bodies and dancing with Divine Reality. Still, a genuinely Christian faith and spirituality recognizes this severed link as nothing less than tragic if it prevents us from embracing a key insight about being created in the image of God: We are erotic creatures because Divine Reality itself is erotic.

The Spirit of divine desire at work in creation, expressing the divine longing for communion, animates us as restless creatures of desire, seeking to express our own longing for the intimate dance for which we were made. In this sense, the many painful and violent distortions of human eroticism, rather than urging us to avoid the erotic, invite us into a more sustained engagement with these powerful energies for the sake of joining the dance.

Turning again to Rowan Williams, Christian faith and spirituality turns on desire itself:

> Grace, for the Christian believer, is a transformation that depends in large part on knowing yourself to be seen in a certain way: as significant, as wanted. The whole story of creation, incarnation, and our incorporation into the fellowship of Christ's body tells us that *God desires us*. . . . The life of the Christian community has as its rationale—if not invariably its practical reality—the task of teaching us to so order our relations that human beings may see themselves as desired, as the occasion of joy.[3]

The task of "ordering our relations," as Williams puts it, pushes us well beyond the standard notions of forgiveness as an accepted apology or a received act of repentance. This ongoing task invites us into a much more intimate and therefore vulnerable space where nothing less is at stake than whether we can create the genuinely human communities of the dance God intends. In that space, our own longing for communion—so often thwarted by our awkward gaffs, stumbling missteps, or more severely by betrayal—is met by the astonishing realization that we ourselves are occasions for joy and delight. Astonishing, because that's more than we thought possible (many of us would be quite content to think of ourselves as merely adequate or not excessively offensive) and exactly what authentic human thriving requires.

The Spirit created that kind of astonishing space for Jesus' disciples after they closed themselves in a locked room, afraid for their safety, paralyzed by guilt, suffocating on their own treason. Making excuses or mumbling an apology, even acts of penitence fall far short of the mark when one's betrayal shatters the very context in which such acts have any meaning. As Jesus appears among them at that moment—unbidden, unexpected, and without any prompting, cajoling, or pleading on their part—I imagine they realize, perhaps for the first time, that forgiveness means something more than paying or canceling debts; besides, indebtedness only scratches the surface of their predicament. Nor does forgiveness rely on the promise of an amended life or on assurances of living better in the future; they say nothing about such things and even if they had, it could not have undone their betrayal. Rather, forgiveness springs from the desire for the beloved, a desire that gives no thought to terms and conditions but only to being united with the beloved. In any act of divine forgiveness, and just like those disciples to whom Jesus appeared, we reconcile ourselves to the fact of being desirable. And this is the energy and the work of the Holy Spirit, the Divine Breath Jesus shares with his disciples in a moment of piercingly tender intimacy.

Christian spirituality invites us to expect the unexpected, the disruptions of traditional patterns by the wind that blows where it wills, and equally breathtaking moments of intimate reconciliation, of finding ourselves desired. As most Christians realize, putting this hope into practice is frequently fraught with problems, especially when our attempts fall short of the hope that inspired them. In this sense, Christian spirituality also exhibits the restless qualities of hope itself, which will not allow us to settle into anything less than the kind of communion both God and we deeply desire. Putting this in another way, if the help we need from the Spirit begins with disruption and leads us into the intimacy of reconciliation, this same Spirit does not then simply rest. To the contrary, spiritual disciplines inevitably generate a lingering restlessness. And this, too, is the work of the Divine Wind, the Intimate Breath, the Spirit Christians insist on calling Holy.

DIVINE RESTLESSNESS

The dynamic and intimate energy of a tango keeps us enthralled even though we never see its eroticism consummated. The energy of desire itself keeps us on the edge of our seats, captivated by the rhythm of the music and the fluid motion of the dance steps. We know where such energy eventually leads. Mainstream Hollywood movies usually show us exactly where it leads, leaving virtually nothing to the imagination. And yet, objecting to explicit displays of sexuality in the movies as thinly veiled moments of pornography overlooks a much more potent avenue of critique.

The quick and often facile consummation of erotic energy in many of today's films usually short-circuits the desire the characters have been fueling throughout the story, which can leave audiences wondering whether there isn't something more to this whole business called sex. The standard objections to explicit sexuality actually miss the point. It is not the sex act itself to which our objections belong but to the implication that such an act can really satisfy the desire that prompted it. The narrative arc of a romantic movie frequently reaches its climax with the climax of the sexual encounter, as if there is nothing more to be said or done about erotic energy. Of course, many Hollywood producers and directors simply give their audiences what they think those audiences want; this in turn shapes the expectations of the audience, both for what happens on the silver screen and what they think ought to happen in their own lives. Given these expectations, we should not be so surprised by the simultaneous obsession and confusion over sexuality in modern Western societies; cultural forces have trained us to pursue quick satisfaction for a desire that cannot be quickly satisfied.

In contrast to such quick fixes stands the tango. As the music and the rhythm intensify, we soon begin to realize how much more is transpiring between the dancers than can be expressed or consummated by what they do once they leave the dance floor. The energy of seduction between them clearly leads somewhere. Still, as the dance unfolds it seems likely that the restlessness of this energy will not be easily or quickly exhausted. The same thing applies to dancing with Divine Reality.

The restlessness in Christian spirituality derives from the energy of hope itself, which is never quite satisfied with how things presently stand. This perpetual dissatisfaction appears in any number of contexts, whether with reference to simple answers offered for difficult questions, or to stale bureaucracies of the institutional church, or to intractable social structures thwarting the process of genuine human thriving. The energy of hope refuses to find any satisfying rest in these systems and structures. While Christian faith clearly leads us somewhere, just as the energy of a tango does, it continually provokes suspicion of tidy resolutions or quick fixes.

Anglican Christians encounter restless hope nearly every time we try to identify what it really means to be an Anglican. Anglicans usually find such reflection either frustrating or embarrassing, yet only rarely is the energy in those moments identified as the Divine Wind, that breath of God called the Holy Spirit. Biblical sources can help here too, especially by turning to the peculiar bridge between the Gospel of Luke and the Acts of the Apostles where divine restlessness appears a bit more explicitly.

Many Christians tend to forget or have failed to notice that the same author wrote both Luke and Acts. The order in which those biblical texts have been arranged obscures that link because the Gospel of John appears between Luke and Acts. Skipping over John, we can see more clearly how the Acts of the Apostles continues the story begun in Luke, with the intention of describing what happened among the disciples after the resurrection of Jesus. The bridge between these books proves both awkward and dramatic, as the author has to figure out what to do, so to speak, with the risen Jesus. The story of Jesus appears to have reached its climax and the disciples' story needs to take some important new turns. The turning point occurs in the ascension, that moment when Jesus exits the stage to make a bit more room for the Spirit. Luke, in other words, needs to create some breathing space on the dance floor of his story; he does so with an ascending Jesus.

The ascension of Jesus, as Luke describes it, usually provokes more incredulity than his resurrection. The image of Jesus being "lifted up" and ascending into the clouds starts to resemble a hokey Hollywood screenplay; at the very least, it reinforces the idea of "heaven" as a realm to which one could actually fly. Apart from those reasonable perplexities, we might think more simply in terms of plot and story line: The Ascension provides a way to wrap up some of the story's loose ends. What happens next, however, is far from tidy.

On the brink of ascending, Jesus instructs his disciples to wait in Jerusalem for the story's next chapter to unfold (Acts 1:4). There they find themselves caught up in a dramatic encounter with Divine Reality on the day of Pentecost, an ancient Jewish festival for celebrating a spring harvest. On that day, according to Luke, the disciples experienced the sound of a rushing wind in the room in which they had gathered and something like flames of fire appeared above their heads. One of the results of this encounter resembles what happens in sessions of the United Nations' General Assembly when a speaker's words are instantly translated into dozens of other languages. Likewise on Pentecost, the disciples were suddenly able to speak in languages they had never studied and began preaching to the crowds in Jerusalem, who had come from all over the empire for the festival. Each of these visitors heard the message in his or her native tongue. If this were not enough, what the disciples said prompted mass conversions. As Luke tells it, three thousand were baptized that very day (Acts 2:41).

At this point, those newly energized disciples could have settled into the business of building a community from these many converts. They could have set up shop in Jerusalem and devised some kind of action plan or mission statement. They clearly started to do these things, but the energy of Pentecost proved far more restless than that. Luke constructs his story in Acts with ever widening circles of encounter, which included conflicts with both religious and Roman authorities, controversies over the presence of Gentiles, contested opinions concerning proper spiritual practices, and missionary journeys reaching far beyond the confines of Palestine. Moments of satisfying clarity or religious nesting in this story are few and far between, which Luke anticipates early on in the way he describes the Pentecost event itself.

Consider how Luke constructs what transpires in that event and recall that the disciples who had gathered together most likely spoke either Hebrew or Aramaic as their native tongue. When the Divine Wind blew through that room, they were moved to preach to foreign visitors in Jerusalem for whom Aramaic was decidedly not their native tongue. What happened next in a startling moment of linguistic comprehension could have transpired in one of two ways. The disciples could have preached in their own language and all those foreign visitors could have quite suddenly understood Aramaic, even if they had never studied it. But that's not how Luke tells it. Instead, the disciples spoke in a number of languages they had never studied so that all those visitors heard the good news in their own native tongue.

This subtle but important difference implies something rather remarkable about how the divine dance unfolds. The foreigners visiting Jerusalem that day were not forced to give up the language of their childhood in order to hear the invitation to dance with God. They heard it spoken in the language they had first heard as infants from their mothers and fathers. Now, quite honestly, this process isn't quite as efficient as I usually prefer. My own inclination toward orderliness would have orchestrated something a bit less cacophonous. Rather than everyone speaking a bunch of different languages, everyone speaking the very same language would sound a bit more pleasing to the ear.

The Holy Spirit, however, doesn't seem particularly interested in what makes sense to us or in constructing orderly plots or maximizing efficiency. If the Acts of the Apostles is any indication, the Holy Spirit entices and seduces us into a dance we might not otherwise have found attractive. When the diversity of the dancers creates discomfort or disrupts the possibility of dancing together at all, the Holy Spirit creates surprising new ways to join the dance, ways we probably could not have imagined on our own.

As Anglican Christians today live with a truly diverse and multicultural worldwide communion, questions not only of Anglican identity but also and more generally of Christian identity are creating increased tension and, for some, a sense of crisis. The tension itself represents nothing terribly new in the history of Christianity and, if Luke's account provides any guidance, we ought not to expect tidy resolutions to those questions any time soon. In fact, we ought to expect precisely the opposite.

As the Divine Wind blows where it wills, breathing fresh life into our systems and institutions and creating the kind of intimacy from which genuine reconciliation springs, we have plenty of reasons to expect a restless energy at work in Christian spirituality and in our institutional life. This does not mean that every instance of restlessness automatically or by definition indicates an encounter with Divine Reality. Distinguishing between genuinely hopeful and merely chaotic energy involves a deliberate and shared process of discernment and the willingness to sustain that process over time. Just as it did for the earliest Christian communities, this process will include regular irruptions of controversy and moments of disagreement and uncertainty. By the same token, we have likely misunderstood or neglected the purpose of Christian spirituality if our engagement with Christian traditions and our participation in the institutional church feels comfortable, settled, and securely rooted. No less than the tango, the restless energy of divine seduction urges us forward, away from our standard zones of comfort and into breathing spaces on the dance floor we have not yet explored.

By rooting spiritual discernment in common prayer, Anglican Christians invoke this restless energy every time we gather to celebrate the Eucharist. Historically, the focus in the eucharistic prayer falls on the "words of institution," the words Jesus spoke concerning the bread and the wine at the last supper he shared with his friends. What comes next in the traditional eucharistic pattern, when the community calls upon the Holy Spirit, deserves just as much attention. In that moment, the eucharistic Jesus reminds us that we ourselves are the body of Christ, driven together by the Divine Wind, sharing a divinely intimate breath.

I often wonder, as I stand at that eucharistic table, if any of us really has any idea of what we're doing when we invoke that Spirit, whether we sense the risk it poses to our comfort and safety, and if we realize the extent to which we are being seduced into a dance that could sweep us off our feet. Annie Dillard, an American poet and essayist, sounds a similar note of caution quite pointedly when she wonders whether Christians realize what could happen in our liturgies when we so blithely call upon the Divine Wind. Perhaps we have forgotten what happened on Pentecost or, as Dillard suspects, we don't really believe it:

The churches are children playing on the floor with their chemistry sets, mixing up a batch of TNT to kill a Sunday morning. It is madness to wear ladies' straw hats and velvet hats to church; we should be wearing crash helmets. Ushers should issue life preservers and signal flares; they should lash us to our pews. For the sleeping god may wake someday and take offense, or the waking god may draw us to where we can never return.[4]

I suppose we can be thankful that divine seduction occurs gradually, yet we can't be sure it always will. The Divine Wind appears unexpectedly, unbidden and uncontrolled. The Divine Breath takes us by surprise with a shocking intimacy. The history of Christian community called "church" exhibits a gradual evolution of the dance, yet it is punctuated by breathtaking moments of transformation. The breathing space offered in Anglican traditions creates an opportunity to reflect on what that kind of religious history means for "being church" today and the kind of hope it inspires us to practice.

6

THE VIRGINIA REEL
~Visions of Unrealized Communion~

Growing up as a religious bookworm, I hated grade-school gym class. While my father thought I possessed the hand-eye coordination to be a baseball player, I preferred to put that talent to use with pen and paper (just as my father did). To me, sports was just a tedious distraction and gym class an occasion for looking foolish.

Twice every year my disdain over this interruption in the rhythm of the classroom turned to anxiety when gym class was devoted to physical fitness evaluations based on federally devised assessment standards. For a Midwestern, middle-class kid like me, this was the most visible manifestation of an otherwise mysterious entity called "government." Virtually unaware of the many and diverse responsibilities our elected officials manage every day, I assumed from these evaluations that our government devoted a great deal of its time and energy to the physical fitness of our country's youth. So as my classmates and I performed chin-ups, push-ups, and sit-ups (or at least made valiant attempts to do so), the image of our gym teacher dutifully making notes on his clipboard kicked my childhood imagination into high gear. I pictured a government bureaucrat sitting in a faraway Washington office carefully reading a stack of physical fitness reports, clucking and shaking his head when he came to mine. I even wondered whether I would eventually receive a special-delivery letter from our nation's capital, scolding me

for my poor performance and urging me to take more seriously my responsibilities as a physically fit American citizen.

Gym class was not, however, uniformly dreadful. On occasion team
sports were replaced by folk dancing. The basketballs, baseball bats, and soc-
cer nets were stored away and in their place a record player appeared on the
raised stage at the far end of the gymnasium. Our regular gym teacher, a
man, was likewise replaced on those occasions with a folk dance instructor,
a woman. This shift in activity and instructor always took us by surprise. We
never knew before arriving at gym class whether we would be shooting
hoops or dancing in squares. For me, my mood changed dramatically and
with a profound sense of relief whenever I walked into that gymnasium and
saw the record player.

Pairing off in couples for square dancing always felt a bit awkward for
children our age, but less so whenever we learned a contra dance, like the
Virginia reel. Contra dances are so named because of the configuration of
the dancers; the men line up one side and the women on the other, facing
the men. While the Virginia reel creates clearly identified couples, each man
actually dances briefly with each of the women. The couples then take turns
"reeling" down the space between the two lines of dancers, who raise their
arms to create a human canopy over the space. This arrangement is not necessarily ideal, especially if the lineup of dancers includes someone you don't
particularly want to dance with, however briefly. Yet that's part of what I
found so intriguing, as I would sometimes notice two schoolyard bullies,
ordinarily at each other's throats during recess, standing next to each other
and participating in a communal dance.

In retrospect I recognize both of these childhood activities—physical fitness assessments and folk dancing—as tools for shaping America's school
children into responsible adults. Yet the difference I experienced between
these two tools could not have been more pronounced. The assessments
scrutinized my level of individual fitness; the dancing invited me to participate in social bonding. I experienced the same difference by leaving the
religious tradition of my childhood to become an Episcopalian. My understanding of worship changed from assessment to participation.

I feel confident that the preachers I heard growing up preached the
gospel as good news, but that's not how I remember hearing it. Going to my
childhood church on Sunday mornings felt like the religious version of under-
going physical fitness assessments and God was the ultimate government

bureaucrat reading the reports. To be sure, I heard a lot about divine forgiveness in that church, but this promise of good news correlated directly with my individual spiritual fitness, which I dutifully tried to assess every Sunday morning. I imagine everyone else in that cavernous church building felt the same way. Being together in that space was somehow incidental to the true task at hand: measuring up to standards.

Worshipping in an Episcopal church literally changed my life, yet it took some time for me to realize why. On the surface, the standards for spiritual fitness in my newfound religious home appeared no less exacting on Sunday mornings, especially as every liturgy included a confession of sin. Before long, however, I realized an important difference. As I fumbled my way through when to stand and when to kneel and which book to pick up from the pew rack and how to move forward gracefully to the altar rail to receive Communion, I experienced a significant shift in perception. I finally realized that being together on a Sunday morning was not merely incidental to our purpose in gathering in that space. Whatever it was we thought we were doing in the liturgy, we were doing it together, and what we did together could not be accomplished on our own.

Over time, walking into that tiny Episcopal parish and seeing its linen-draped granite altar prompted the same kind of feeling I had walking into my grade-school gymnasium and seeing a record player on the stage. The feeling in both cases was one of profound relief. Here, I realized, in this church, I was being invited into something rather than trying to measure up to something. And this "something" into which I was being invited incorporated movement and graceful lines and vibrant colors and sweet-smelling scents. I was being invited into the company of dancers, asked only to dance as best I could. Whether I danced well or stumbled through it mattered far less than being swept off my feet into the motion of divine grace in a way I had not nor could not experience in the privacy of my own home.

Describing liturgical experience in this way clearly taps into romantic if not idealized notions of a worshipping community. The weekly liturgy of any given congregation doesn't always feel quite so energizing; it sometimes plods along, ponderous, rote, and even lifeless. Still, and historically speaking, Anglicans have rooted their sense of Christian identity in institutional forms of common prayer, which tend to blend together the activity called liturgy and the institution called church. This is not to say Anglicans ignore individual devotional practice. Rather, we tend to understand our corporate liturgical life as the deep roots of our faith from which the individual branches receive their nourishment; without those roots, the branches cannot bear fruit. The religious tradition of my childhood tended to reverse that dynamic between roots and branches. I grew up perceiving my own individual religious practices as the deep roots of my faith; if I tended them properly, they would bear fruit at Sunday morning worship. Embracing Anglican Christianity thus proved both startling and liberating: The roots of Christian faith lay deep in the gathered community and I was no longer solely responsible for tending them.

In retrospect, my early experiences with folk dancing helped prepare me for making this shift in perception occasioned by becoming an Episcopalian. Nearly every culture practices some kind of communal choreography to express its cultural or ethnic ties, or to celebrate a religious festival, or to pass on acquired wisdom. Moreover, while folk dances, especially contra dances, are structured with couples, they are not designed for the purpose of coupling. Instead, they serve to nurture the bonds of the larger community. Folk dances encourage communal cohesion, which is precisely why we learned them in grade school.

At times, the desire to create and maintain strong social ties is fueled by "outside" influences, especially if the influences are perceived as a threat to the community's life. In response to such a threat, communal cohesion can turn rather quickly to communal conformity and even communal coercion for the sake of sustaining the community's identity. Like folk dancing, institutional Christian liturgy serves social and communal cohesion and it has historically exhibited the same kind of troubling turns to both conformity and coercion, to which Anglican Christians have devoted a rather peculiar kind of energy and attention. Our Roman Catholic cousins tend to locate their liturgical life in centralized institutional authority, which reached its zenith in the nineteenth-century declaration of papal infallibility. Free-church Protestantism, on the other hand, tends to abandon traditional institutional structures in favor of more localized congregational expressions and often with a view toward recovering "pure and simple" biblical Christianity.

Anglican Christians have at times veered toward the safety of institutional conformity and, at others, toward a nostalgic longing for "primitive" Christianity. Yet neither of these trajectories gains much traction among Anglicans over time. Instead, Anglican communities inhabit a perpetually restless institutional space where the bond between liturgical action and corporate structure remains both strong and remarkably malleable. This restless tension does not usually inspire either relational comfort or clarity of vision, but it can inspire hope. The typically Anglican refusal to centralize institutional authority or to circumscribe liturgical practice can animate visions of a genuinely communal dance with God.

Today, as religious institutions undergo increasingly critical scrutiny (and rightly so, in many cases), putting Anglican forms of Christian hope into practice requires a particular kind of liturgical and institutional vigilance. The temptation to resolve definitively our Anglican restlessness remains as strong today as it was in sixteenth- and seventeenth-century England. Yet much more is at stake here than whether an Anglican identity admits any precise definitions. The peculiarly Anglican flavor of this ongoing conversation reflects a much broader concern with which Christian communities have lived from the very beginning. This concern cuts to the heart of making Christian faith a matter of truly good news: How can we dance with God, not merely on our own, but together?

Responding to that question leads into a two-sided exploration of what church means and what it means to "be church." This kind of exploration involves, first, examining the relationship between religion and culture and how the various forms of that relationship shape perceptions of church, or what we could describe as "the cultural music of religion." In addition to the influences of culture, explorations of church also involve a consideration of the relationship between the texts of a religious institution and the actual religious practices of the institution's members. The general tendency to think of religious texts as instruction manuals for the life of faith fails to take into account how faithful practice actually shapes and informs the texts and their development. Many of today's controversies over how to "be church" have their roots in an excessive reliance on the texts of our traditions at the expense of any reflection on how communities actually practice their faith— a dynamic we could refer to as the "textual rhythm of church."

Exploring these two features of institutional forms of church reorients some of today's ecclesiastical controversies in more helpful directions. They serve as a reminder that the rules of a given choreography are for the sake of the dance itself. This is the case for Anglican theological method generally and especially in how Anglicans shape institutional church life and the priorities we set for that life. Rather than trying to maintain institutional church structures for their own sake, Anglicans try to remember that those structures are perpetually provisional, always pointing beyond themselves to visions of as yet unrealized communion. This is the same hope inspired by the Virginia reel—to discern the choreography for a genuinely communal dance.

THE CULTURAL MUSIC OF RELIGION

Folk dances retain traces of their cultural history of which contemporary dancers are often unaware. I was quite surprised, for example, to learn about the origins of "Ring around the Rosey," which I had danced to as a young child. That children's dance has its roots in the devastation of bubonic plague in medieval Europe. Coming to that realization opened up a new and a somewhat macabre world of meaning for the familiar words I had learned at such a tender age: "Ashes, ashes, we all fall down!" Likewise, the style of contra dancing we refer to as the Virginia reel did not in fact originate in Virginia but in France and England. (Not surprisingly, both the French and the English claim to have invented it.)

Religious institutions also have cultural histories, which continue to shape various approaches to theology, liturgical movements, leadership structures, styles of ecclesiastical garb and vestment, and ethical norms and models. These cultural roots run deep in religious traditions, which relatively few Christians stop to consider in the assumptions they make about the relationship between religious values and cultural values. I grew up with a picture of the institutional church as somehow distinct from its various historical contexts, set apart from and above the messy flow of cultural development. More than just distinct, I understood "religion" to be in competition with "culture" without ever considering the extent to which my conceptions of religious faith had been deeply molded by my own cultural assumptions. Picturing Jesus as vaguely Scandinavian is just one example among many. The "scandalous" practice of women wearing makeup is another, as well as the fact that our church building was designed to look like a lecture hall. Becoming an Episcopalian merely shifted these cultural influences toward older historical sources, but those sources were firmly planted in cultural influences nonetheless.

Instead of floating free from or somehow above the shifting currents of cultural change and development, both Christian theology and ethics give particular expression to the many overlapping layers of attitude, behavior, and custom referred to as "culture." Christian faith may respond to culture—in the form of critical analysis or as a source of insight—but religion and culture are nevertheless interwoven with each other in nearly organic fashion; discerning where one ends and the other begins is virtually impossible.

The dynamic blend of religion and culture lends added texture and complexity to hearing divine music, learning its choreography, and stepping foot on the dance floor of faith. Each of these elements in dancing with God, just like our interactions with the institutional church, is firmly planted in cultural histories. Dancing well entails giving at least some consideration to the cultural and institutional formation of the dance.

The texts of the Hebrew scriptures, for example, come from a theocratic society in which there was no distinction worth making between religion and culture. But the ancient Israelites themselves would not have referred to their society as theocratic any more than the ancient Egyptians or Babylonians would have. Theocracy has meaning only in contrast to societies that separate religious faith from civic governance, an idea those ancient societies would have found perplexing at best. As the Hebrew prophets describe it, the moments of crisis Israel faced usually erupted after Israel abandoned religious faith as its guiding principle in structuring society. Reading those texts requires a careful consideration of whether they point to a theological insight or represent traces of ancient Mesopotamian cultural custom; more often than not, such texts incorporate both.

The texts of the Christian scriptures, on the other hand, come from communities in which Israelite theocracy had taken on a whole new level of complexity in relation to Greco-Roman culture. Both the gospels and Paul's letters emerge not from a seamless union of religion and culture but from the untidy intersections among ancient Israelite religion, a new and barely gestated form of religious faith focused on Jesus of Nazareth, and the politics and philosophies of the Roman Empire. In those communities, questions of religious faith emerged as much from their confrontations with particular cultural practices as they did from concerns over theology; more often than not, they were a blend of both.

Theological texts from the earliest centuries of subsequent Christian thought and practice come from an era of cultural persecution by the Roman Empire, whereas later texts, after Constantine's conversion to Christianity, come from an era of cultural embrace. Some centuries after that, with the collapse of the Roman Empire and the emergence of medieval European society, a new kind of wedding between religion and culture took place. But this wasn't merely a European version of an ancient Israelite theocracy. If the Israelites understood "culture" as the concrete expression of their religious faith, medieval Europeans tended to reverse this relationship: Institutional forms of religion became the way to express and enact particular cultural developments. The galvanizing image of the Pope crowning Charlemagne as emperor of the new and now "Holy" Roman Empire in the year 800 is just one among many examples.

When we consider the appearance of Europeans on the American continent, new kinds of complexity come into play: New England is settled by English Puritans; the southeastern seaboard by Church of England colonists; the Mississippi Delta by French missionaries; and the West Coast by Spanish conquistadors. European culture, in other words, is established on the American continent with reference to particular religious traditions. And here something truly revolutionary occurred. The untidy edges of this religious colonization were not sewn together by establishing more securely the link between religion and culture. Precisely the opposite happened. The United States is sewn together by disestablishing religion and by enshrining the distinction between religious practice and civic governance in its founding political document.

Disentangling what "religion" means from what "culture" means in this long and varied history from ancient to modern contexts proves daunting at best if not actually impossible. Religious communities have always danced to particular types of cultural music. Even social policy in the United States, which is supposedly constructed within the framework of the "separation of church and state," has been historically shaped by explicitly religious sensibilities. The civil rights movement of the 1960s was not only fueled by religious rhetoric and shaped by religious leaders (such as Martin Luther King Jr.), it was also responding to the racial inequities that had been informed in no small measure by equally religious postures and attitudes.

The worldwide Anglican Communion has only just begun to confront the legacy of European cultural music in the churches of Africa, Asia, and South America. As the colonial reach of the British empire gradually withered in the eighteenth and nineteenth centuries, a particular form of ecclesial relation appeared among the churches left behind in those former colonies. Each national region or province in those colonial outposts began to enjoy its own autonomy while still maintaining a link to the Church of England. Anglicans refer to this loosely construed link and all the historical ties it evokes as "being in communion with the Archbishop of Canterbury."

It is by no means clear, however, to what extent English cultural music plays well in all these religious communities so far flung from London. More than just styles of worship and institutional structure, the content of Christian theology itself comes under scrutiny in postcolonial conversations about whether the good news of Christian faith can be distinguished from its European cultural expressions. To what extent has the "portable Jesus" blended seamlessly with Western (European) cultural values? How is the Spirit shaping our communal dance and with what kind of steps? What does it mean to "be church" in the midst of complex cultural diversity? Njongonkulu Ndungane, the Anglican Archbishop of Cape Town, points to the history of these questions on the African continent and describes it as the attempt to

> dress Christianity in African culture while maintaining its foreignness in terms of symbols, thought forms and value systems. In practice this implied the adaptation of European practices and thought patterns to the cultural life of the people of Africa. Even more objectionable is the assumption that scripture has independence from the culture in which it is read, and therefore has authority over African traditions and values. The use of scripture to legitimize africanisation of Christianity was an attempt to impose European domination and control upon Africa.[1]

Ndungane is not suggesting that Anglicans abandon any authority for Christian scripture and traditions in Africa or anywhere else. Rather, he wants to examine who does the work of interpreting those traditions in various cultural contexts. In the past, European colonial missionaries tried to do that work. Today theological reflection needs all the voices in Africa working together, including missionaries, local people, women, and men. Both traditional and contemporary symbols and interpretations are needed, Ndungane notes, but not for a "single definitive version of contextualized Christianity. There will be as many variations as there are influences and voices."[2]

Anglican traditions have already lived through the contexualization Ndungane describes. The sixteenth-century English Reformation is just one example. Medieval Catholic traditions combined with and transformed by insights from Protestant reformers on the Continent produced a particular kind of cultural music with some peculiar dance steps in English churches. The peculiarity of those steps illustrates what has always been the case in

Christian history: Christian communities continually engage in the work of contextualizing their faith. This task is enshrined in the biblical texts themselves, witnessed by the Apostle Paul's attempts to translate theological insights about Jesus into the particular contexts of Greco-Roman culture.

Today, the history of decentralizing Anglican authority and liturgical practice, especially in concert with the forces of globalization and mass communication, has sparked new controversies in the Anglican Communion and deepened old ones. These controversies are fueling a centuries-old Anglican perplexity about what it really means to be "in communion" with each other, most notably but not exclusively with reference to the ordination of women and the presence of openly gay and lesbian clergy. The hope of dancing with God together, even in the midst of controversy and disagreement, represents nothing terribly new in the history of Christianity, but each generation must put that hope into practice in new ways. Addressing that challenge involves dealing not only with how cultural music shapes religious faith but also with the equally complex relationship between the texts of a religious institution and the actual religious practices of the institution's members. Simply put, what kind of role should theological texts play in the practice of Christian faith?

THE TEXTUAL RHYTHM OF CHURCH

Both ballroom-style dancing, like the tango, and folk dancing, like the Virginia reel, tend to blur the otherwise clear distinctions between leaders and followers in the dance. Sometimes the "leader" in a tango actually needs to follow the urgings of the "follower" to find some breathing space on the dance floor. Likewise, while the Virginia reel clearly distinguishes leaders and followers, each of the dancers winds up dancing with all the others. A similar dynamic appears in the ongoing task any religious community must face in shaping its conduct of life from the insights gleaned in religious and theological texts. My own inclination in such matters resembles how I approach computer skills. I read the manual and try to follow what the text says about what to do with the mouse and the keyboard. But I often learn much more by actually putting those instructions into practice, which can in turn shape how I read the manual. This dynamic exchange between text and practice has influenced institutional church life in some complex and surprising ways.

I suspect most people, religious and nonreligious alike, imagine religious leaders (the clergy) guiding religious followers (lay people) around the religious dance floor as they nudge them with biblical texts and theological doctrines. Over time, life in the church blurs those distinctions considerably. Reflection on religious leading and following most often appears whenever the diversity of God's people raises questions about the unity of God's people. In Anglican history, the Elizabethan Settlement in sixteenth-century England tried to address the violent diversity between Protestants and Catholics, which involved questions of political allegiance to the Crown as much as debates over theological integrity. The solution to the threat of a divided kingdom took the form of common prayer in public, the adoption of the Book of Common Prayer, and various acts of Parliament regarding religious conformity. The stress in this solution fell squarely on the public character of the settlement, which held virtually no implications for what Christians actually did or believed in private. Queen Elizabeth herself reportedly remarked that she had no intention of policing individual conscience; she cared only for social and political cohesion.

Reflecting on the Elizabethan Settlement raises questions about the relationship between the official texts of a religious institution and the variety of practices exhibited by members of that institution. If we wish to assess sixteenth-century English Christianity, do we turn to the public expressions of an ostensibly "Protestant" form of common prayer or to the private expressions of historically "Catholic" devotional practices? How do we distinguish between religious leaders and religious followers in this case? For those English reformers, public institutional texts were not necessarily leading the religious dance in private. Indeed, the diversity of private practices actually led the institution to devise an adequate compromise in its public texts. This one historical example illustrates the difficulties encountered in turning only to the texts of Christian traditions for discerning the shape of Christian faith.

Institutional church life rarely reduces to the process of applying the insights of texts to the practice of day-to-day conduct, even though Christian communities tend to rely on the textual rhythm of being church as their default position. For both theology and ethics, Christians almost automatically cite authoritative texts—whether from the Bible or from particular theologians—the authority of which the institutional church itself determines. At the same time, this textual rhythm is frequently forged by the way

Christians actually practice their faith, which sixteenth-century Anglicans discovered anew in the Elizabethan Settlement. The texts of theological traditions certainly offer important insights, but they also have limits.

Biblical texts, for example, were frequently written in response to questions raised by the practices of a particular community. By reading Paul's letters to various churches we can make some intelligent guesses about the practices of those communities based on the theological reflection Paul offers in response (compare, for example, 1 Corinthians 8–11 and Galatians 2–3). But we can't know precisely how those communities received his letters, the kind of changes they made or didn't make in their practices, or the extent to which evolving practices shaped and reshaped Paul's theological perspectives.

In these early Christian communities, the theological questions posed by diverse practices almost always led to a complex mix of uniformity and compromise. The incorporation of Gentiles into Christian community was one of the first critical issues faced by Jewish Christians, an issue addressed at the so-called "Council of Jerusalem" recorded in Acts 15. After much debate and passionate pleas by Paul, the council agreed not to "burden" Gentiles with the regimen of ancient Israelite custom, except with reference to refraining from idolatry, sexual immorality, and eating anything that had been strangled (15:19–20).

The challenges early Christians faced extended well beyond diverse practices (like eating meat sacrificed to idols) and into the realm of theological belief. The essence of Christian faith hanging decisively on salvation by grace alone, as it does in Paul's letter to the Galatians, shifts rather dramatically in the letter of James, where faith relies as much'on generating good works as it does on grace (2:14–26). While the letter to the Hebrews turns to notions of priestly sacrifice to describe the saving work of Christ, Paul's letter to the Romans employs the image of Jesus as the "second Adam," whose obedience to God's will reverses the disobedience of the first Adam (5:12–21). Which of these theological perspectives should inform Christian practice today? How did they form the practices of the communities to which those texts were written?

Discerning the relationship between diverse texts and multiple practices in the Bible only grows more complex as we look at the centuries that followed. Consider the challenges in describing fourth-century Christianity, for which it is not enough to cite passages from the work of Augustine or the

Cappadocians. Those texts suggest how theological ideas were developing, but they can't tell us how local Christian communities were praying or actually practicing the faith those texts describe. We can't be sure that the way in which a community on the outskirts of Rome practiced its faith looked exactly like the theology Augustine articulated. We do know that Augustinian choreography has inspired not just one way, but a variety of ways to dance (whether in early medieval Christianity or in its reconfigurations at the hands of Thomas Aquinas or in the revolutionary proposals of Martin Luther or in the theocratic experiments of John Calvin).

Contemporary churches pose similar questions about the relationship between texts and practices. Since the 1960s, official Roman Catholic texts, for example, have forbidden the use of artificial birth control. Many Roman Catholics, especially in the United States, have been virtually ignoring this textual exhortation for quite some time while still attending church and receiving Communion. Hundreds of years from now, when historians try to describe twentieth-century Roman Catholicism, will they turn to the official texts or to the practices of faithful Catholics or to a blend of both? At this stage, and concerning many more issues than just birth control, we cannot yet know how faithful practices will inform the development of institutional texts.

The mutual exchange between texts and practices also operates in the way Christians try to interact with social structures and cultural institutions. For Anglicans, the theological perspectives of F. D. Maurice and William Temple continue to pose questions about the relationship between institutional Christianity and an increasingly pluralistic society. Discerning whether their insights can translate into twenty-first-century contexts raises additional questions about the role theological texts play in the choreography of being church.

Both Maurice and Temple believed the doctrine of the Incarnation holds profound implications for the church's role in society. This is a fairly typical Anglican conviction, especially when working in the Church of England, a religious institution officially established by the State. But textual theological traditions urged them to treat the material conditions and circumstances of society as spiritually relevant in the most fundamental way. Maurice, for example, contributed significantly to the nineteenth-century development of "Christian socialism" by understanding the Incarnation as the theological expression of human society's essential unity. For Maurice, the structure of human society itself manifests the divine order of creation God intends for human beings. Through sustained education and a vigorous repudiation of individualism, Maurice believed the church could make this divine order clear and foster a stronger bond of unity among the stratified social classes of English society.

Unfortunately, Maurice's devotion to this theological insight tended to obscure the severe social animosity and inequities operating in nineteenth-century English culture. The theological insight gleaned from Christian texts seemed to prevent Maurice from making a critical assessment of the very social structures that lay at the root of the problems he sought to address. Temple, working in the early twentieth century, recognized this problem and envisioned a more ambitious role for the church.

Temple, like Maurice, grounded his vision in the far-reaching implications of the Incarnation. Unlike Maurice, Temple understood the Incarnation as the theological mandate for the church to "interfere" in the social policies and structures of human society for the sake of transforming society itself. Throughout his life in the Church of England, including his role as Archbishop of Canterbury, Temple took some bold steps with this vision, such as crafting economic policy recommendations and proposing specific resolutions for labor disputes. Most of these initiatives ultimately failed, due in part to Temple's own lack of expertise in economics and, frankly, a kind of theological naïveté concerning the practical realities of human culture and politics.[3]

The legacy of Maurice's and Temple's work—both their successes and failures—continues to inspire Anglican approaches to the relationship between the institutional church and the secular institutions of society. In the United States, Episcopalians have historically drawn from English establishment roots for their engagements with American social policy, most notably in terms of economics and race relations.[4] Just as significantly, the relationship between the texts of an institutional church and the cultural practices of a given society can prompt renewed scrutiny of the church itself. At times, cultural practices invite a reevaluation of institutional church policies and the theological texts informing those policies. That kind of scrutiny continues to provoke controversy on several fronts, both for Episcopalians in the United States and, more broadly, for Anglicans worldwide. The ordination of women as priests offers a classic case in point.

In the early 1970s, the Episcopal Church had not yet officially admitted women to the ordained priesthood, even after decades of study and theological reflection. In 1974, several courageous bishops decided to push the institution on this question by ordaining eleven equally courageous women as priests before the wider church had approved the practice. As a result, the 1976 General Convention of the Episcopal Church voted to revise its canons on ordination to include women. The threats of schism this decision provoked expressed a longstanding anxiety over the possibility that particular practices would prompt changes in official texts. Those who were and continue to be opposed to the ordination of women were quite correct when they argued that such a step indicated not merely a change in practice but also in theology. Ordaining women to the priesthood has reoriented theological ideas about ministry and leadership, provoked questions about gendered language for God, and even shifted perceptions about the relationship between the sacraments of the church and the hope of salvation.

Those same opponents were mistaken, however, to suppose that theology does not or ought not to change. This assumption derives in part from treating the texts of theology as a stable tradition to which shifting practices must conform. The history of the church reveals a much more dynamic process. Texts and practices exhibit a fluid and mutually affecting relationship in the institutional development of the church, which defies nearly every attempt to identify a definitive textual expression of Christian faith. Practical revisions in church life inevitably recast the idea of church itself just as much as concepts of what it means to "be church" influence how church is practiced.[5]

The evolutionary and frequently unsettled character of church is certainly not new in church history. But we can say more than that. Christian traditions invite us to place our trust in what we call church not because of its supposed stability, but because of what its inherent instability can teach us about dancing with God. Christian faith and theology invite a vision of church as the perpetually unfinished choreography of communion and invite us to treat this vision not merely as something to be tolerated but to be embraced as a source of hope.

THE UNFINISHED CHOREOGRAPHY OF COMMUNION

The various types of dancing correspond to a wide range of ideas and experiences human beings wish to express, not merely in speaking but with our bodies, our bones and muscles. For that reason, throughout the theological explorations in this book, dancing has served simultaneously as a way to think about Christian theology and as a way to reflect on how to put the hope of that theology into practice. Now, however, after moving through some of the classic touchstones in Christian thought and practice, these explorations have arrived on the brink of a rather peculiar and even confounding aspect of Christian traditions with respect to what the concept of "church" really means.

Over time, as Christian theology developed, the idea of church grew beyond the obviously practical concerns any human community faces in devising appropriate organizational structures; the church itself became an article of Christian belief. Evidence of this evolution appears as early as the Council of Nicaea, which most Christians probably overlook whenever they recite the Nicene Creed on Sunday mornings. The Trinitarian pattern of that creed appears clearly enough in its three articles of belief: We believe in God the Creator; we believe in Jesus, the Incarnate Word; we believe in the Holy Spirit, the Giver of Life. But then the music of this creed sounds a remarkable note, a fourth article of belief: "We believe in one, holy, catholic and apostolic church."

I suspect a good number of Christians recite that line in the Nicene Creed without fully realizing its implications. Historic Christian faith invites belief in the church in the same way we believe in Divine Reality. For many, it would be just as strange to suppose that dancing not only expresses various aspects of human life but is also something in which we place our faith and trust. More than a few Christians likely find such notions about church disconcerting at best and probably bordering on the ludicrous. How can we believe in an institution in the same way we believe in God?

Christian traditions have tried to ease our incredulity on this point by turning to christological insights. Just as Jesus represents the union of human and divine, so too the institutional church manifests the incarnate mystery of heaven joined with earth. Anglican theologians have at times attempted to retrieve this traditional insight, as evidenced by some seventeenth-century Anglican scholars known collectively as the Caroline Divines, and later, in the nineteenth-century Oxford Movement. In both cases, these particular Anglicans sought to describe the church not merely as a human institution but also as a manifestation of Divine Reality, of the Trinitarian dance itself. While this approach can sound attractive in theory, which is often referred to as a "high church" perspective, before long many of us probably wonder just how many parish committee meetings these high church scholars attended and how the often tedious and ponderous (if not infuriating) machinations of church politics and conventions reflect anything we want to attribute to divine life. More acutely and significantly, high church theology should be scrutinized in light of the undeniable blunders and tragic missteps the institutional church has made, whether in violent crusades, inquisitional torture, or the shameful support of slavery, to name just a few.

Stretching our credulity to "believe in" the church highlights two key features of Anglican Christianity in some concrete and particular ways. Both human fallibility and the liminal quality of Christian identity find explicit expression in the ongoing disappointments so many of us experience with institutional church life. The experience of disillusionment itself offers an important clue about the practice of Christian hope, the restless qualities of which refuse any facile satisfaction in the way the church presently operates. The severity of disillusionment with the institutional church is directly proportional to the hope the institution generates. When we invest our time and energy in this institution, we do so because of the desire planted in us by God for communion, the desire to give ourselves away in love in our dance with God and with each other. What we see and what we experience in folk dancing, for example, both awakens our hope and expresses that hope for an authentically communal dance. If the choreography of the dance proves disappointing, it does so precisely because we want so much to believe what it tries to express; indeed and in some sense, we want so much to believe in it.

Giving concrete expression to Christian hope is another way of speaking about the sacraments of the church, which likewise pose serious questions. Just like the many texts and creeds of Christian theology, the sacraments run the risk of creating static markers out of something much more dynamic. This risk appears more generally in the impulses experienced outside institutional church life. When we present a birthday gift to a friend or family member, we sometimes worry whether that person will really like it. We worry about it not because the gift itself matters but because we want the gift to express adequately the ongoing relationship we have with that person. Or consider the American celebration of Thanksgiving Day every year late in November. The time off from work, the gathering of friends and families, and the outrageous feast many of us prepare are all meant to express our gratitude for the bounty of life itself. For precisely that reason, Thanksgiving

Day can sometimes prove so terribly disappointing—quarrels erupt among family members, or the roast turkey dries out, or we recall the shameful treatment of Native Americans at the hands of European settlers. Each of these can taint the expression of gratitude as it falls short of the high hopes that prompted it.

Traditionally, sacraments have been understood in much the same way as these more ordinary elements of human life, as concrete and visible expressions of an otherwise ineffable if not unspeakable reality. Baptism, for example, expresses visibly the mysterious claim of being incorporated into the body of Christ, an expression of the particular Jesus becoming portable in us. Likewise the Eucharist, among other things, gives visible expression to the Holy Breath animating the body of Christ with God's own energy of reconciliation. In the same way, the church itself is sacramental, a visible expression of the communal dance into which God invites us all.

The occasional and in some cases ongoing disillusionment that comes with these sacramental aspects of church life derives in large measure from treating these sacraments, including the church, as ends in themselves. Even the word "sacrament" can mislead us when it sounds like a thing, a "holy object," something to revere or venerate for its own sake. The tendency to reify sacraments, to make "things" out of them, has deep and ancient roots in religious history. Just one illustration comes from a pivotal moment in the gospels of Matthew, Mark, and Luke when Jesus' appearance is transfigured in a vision of glory. Peter's impulse at that moment is to build a booth for Jesus and, presumably, preserve the glory. Jesus, however, refused to be preserved as a holy object or treated like a statue on a pedestal (Matthew 17:1–8). If even Jesus won't sit still on that mountaintop, some of the typical assumptions Christians tend to harbor about the church's sacraments probably need revising.

In terms of dancing, I can recall my love of ballet whenever I see posters and newspaper stories advertising the latest dance company production. These marketing tools frequently feature a photograph of a dancer captured in mid-leap, or gracefully poised on the brink of making one. Those images inspire my longing to see the production, but seeing the image cannot possibly satisfy the longing to be swept up and away by the dance itself. When I do attend the performance, there are moments when I wish I could freeze-frame the action or photograph a particularly poignant pas de deux. I want to savor it and hold on to that slice of breathtaking beauty. At the same time,

I know such freeze-framing would fall far short of the experience itself. Similarly, sacraments are "things" to honor only insofar as they provoke our longing for the dance, which cannot be reduced to a static moment. In this sense, life in the church is best understood as sacramental action, a dynamic expression of our longing to join a still unfolding dance.[6]

I misunderstood this kind of energy in liturgical life when I first became an Episcopalian. As someone new to an explicitly sacramental tradition, I assumed the communal reverence I witnessed in church rightly applied to the sacraments themselves. This view is not entirely mistaken, I realized, but not quite adequate either. I experienced a subtle but significant shift in perception on this point by singing a traditional eucharistic hymn, the text of which I initially found a bit troubling. In the midst of the communal piety in my home parish, reverently kneeling in our pews after receiving Communion, we sang these words: "So, Lord, at length when sacraments shall cease, may we be one with all thy Church above."

When sacraments shall cease? That sounded quite odd indeed and I didn't understand. I thought receiving the sacrament was the point of gathering around that table in the first place. "More blessed still," the hymn concluded, "in peace and love to be, one with the Trinity in unity."[7] That's when it dawned on me: Even the Eucharist points beyond itself to an as-yet-unrealized communion.

Eucharistic liturgical styles vary considerably in the Anglican Communion, ranging from elaborate, highly stylized ceremonial to streamlined, sparse gestures and vestments. On occasion, some congregations will also incorporate a celebration of the Eucharist into a larger, more substantial meal. Mostly, and regardless of style, Christians receive only a small piece of bread and a tiny sip of wine at the eucharistic table. And that's exactly how it should be. As I realized when I sang that eucharistic hymn, the Eucharist is not supposed to satisfy us. Even though the word Eucharist means thanksgiving, it's not supposed to make us feel the way many Americans do after feasting on our late-November Thanksgiving Day meal. Rather than providing satisfaction, the Eucharist is supposed to awaken our desire and sharpen our hunger—not just for more bread and more wine, but our desire for God and our hunger for intimacy, our yearning fully to join the dance. The mere nibble we receive at the eucharistic table can remind us that God's abundant life has not yet arrived in its fullness and that the choreography for divine communion is far from finished. The same perspective applies to each of the other sacramental actions we undertake as church, including our enactment of what it means to be church.

Fierce debates in the church and about the church among Anglican Christians can and do sometimes derive from superficial and even petty aspirations for institutional power and control. Upon closer scrutiny, even the most crass political machinations can point to a deeper theological insight. Rather than merely tolerating the Anglican tendency to argue and disagree, embracing the unsettled qualities of institutional church life can serve as a reminder of what we want the church to express—even if the church falls short of doing so, which it inevitably will. Just like our participation in the Eucharist, life in the church is not supposed to satisfy us; precisely the opposite. It's supposed to awaken our restless hope for that to which the church can only haltingly point.

Carefully defined doctrines and perfectly crafted liturgies will always fall short of the hope that inspired them. It is the restless energy of that hope and the courageous faith such hope inspires that make us church, a people who insist on hoping for more than we can now see. As the biblical writer reminds us, "faith is the assurance of things hoped for, the conviction of things not seen" (Hebrews 11:1). By definition, lasting satisfaction cannot come from fallible and liminal attempts to put that kind of hope into practice. The perpetually unsettled and at times turbulent relations in the worldwide Anglican Communion can express and actually give voice to the good news of Christian faith: There is still more to hope for in our dance with God.

Living together as church relies on what we cannot yet see clearly. The choreography of communion remains unfinished, just as Christian theological ideas constantly invite reevaluation and revision. This should not be surprising if experiences with dancing prove at all illuminating. Learning how to waltz the two-step recast my relationship to the rules of theological reflection by making the dance itself a priority rather than the rules. Trusting the dance floor to support me even when I am unsure of the steps urges me to consider faith as a matter of courage rather than of certainty. Turning to the help of a community to hear divine music makes the practice of a Trinitarian faith just as important as trying to figure out how to speak about it. Encountering the divine breath of the eucharistic Jesus regulates my own bodily breathing to the rhythms of a salvation still unfolding. In all of these ways and more, the hope of dancing with God encourages and compels bold experimentation with the traditions we have inherited from communities just as fallible and liminal as our own.

As the music plays and the dancers lift their arms to make a canopy of blessing, the Virginia reel can stir a deep longing. As each couple, newly constituted with every turn, whirls and reels down the avenue of communal embrace, they offer a glimpse of the desire at the heart of the universe. This glimpse, of course, proves short-lived when the music ends; but the longing itself lingers in visions of unrealized communion. Encountering Divine Reality in church and with church and as church can likewise exhilarate and disappoint at the same time. By becoming an Anglican Christian, I learned to recognize that quality of church life, not as a barrier to practicing my Christian faith but rather as one of the key reasons why Christian faith qualifies as genuinely good news—there is always more for which we can hope. As I have come to discover over the years, and often in surprising ways, reflecting on encounters with Divine Reality with the tools and insights of Anglican traditions, even in all their peculiar idiosyncrasies and historical faults and foibles, can still inspire the practice of hope.

PROSPECTS FOR THE DANCE
~ Hopeful Wallflowers
and Postmodern Anglicans~

Christian communities have been engaged in the art and discipline of theology for many centuries. After so much time and energy spent on listening for the music, studying the choreography, and practicing the steps, we might expect by now to have a clear vision of what it looks like to dance with God. Today, more than two thousand years after the birth of Jesus, we might expect to see a beautifully choreographed, harmonious Christian dance, which everyone is eager to join. This is clearly not the case. If anything, Christian faith seems even more perplexing today than it was thirty, even twenty years ago. That's not how I remember the Christianity of my childhood.

Back then, praying and going to church just felt natural and normal and Christian faith made sense. The Bible told us what to believe and how to live. My family and friends knew what it meant to be a Christian and everyone with whom we went to church believed exactly the same thing we did. Human history was a single story with a clearly defined beginning, middle, and end. The many nations of the world divided distinctly between Christian and non-Christian; Americans belonged quite securely to the former. That's how I remember it, even though the world and religious faith were much more complex than that, even then.

Today, the complexities have grown exponentially. Dancing with God now transpires on a barely recognizable dance floor, the edges of which have blurred. The global religious landscape of a twenty-first-century world defies any precise mapping. Both the diversity of religious traditions and the diversity within a single religious tradition resist adequate generalization. Fundamentalist forms of religious faith, whether in Islam or Christianity, continue to grow rapidly in some quarters, while other parts of the world eschew any attachment at all to religious practices. The religious landscape in the United States now exhibits a "post-denominational" topography; loyalty to a particular tradition matters far less than the qualities and energy of a local congregation. Some go further and describe contemporary American society as increasingly "post-Christian," marked by emerging faith communities that blend various religious traditions in novel ways. Clear lines between the religious and nonreligious have virtually disappeared while the number of spiritualities detached from any recognizably religious institution continues to grow.

In the midst of these complex demographics, some people are making tentative steps back into traditionally mainline Christian churches. They are moved to do so perhaps from a nostalgic longing for their childhood faith, or as a way to respond to a somewhat vague, maybe even explicit desire for community, or for a sense of belonging to something larger than themselves. Some are simply curious but a bit wary of religious institutions and of "organized religion" generally. I imagine this diverse and growing population as the "wallflowers" at the dance of Christian faith, and they're hopeful. They have taken the courageous step of showing up at the dance, but they stay on the edges, unwilling to commit to the choreography too quickly.

The small mission congregation where I attend church attracts a good number of these wallflowers and many of them show up quite regularly on Sunday mornings. Some of them grew up in the kind of fundamentalist church where Christian faith sounded more restrictive than expansive and rather far removed from what they would consider "good news." For them, some of the traditional language we continue to use on Sunday mornings triggers unhappy memories. Others grew up without any religious faith at all and they have begun to wonder whether Christianity might offer that "something" (they're not sure what) they seem to be missing. For them, religious faith sounds intriguing and holds potential, but they don't want a fairytale God or to listen to strings of platitudes and moralistic diatribes from the pulpit. Some of them bring insights from other religious traditions with them. Some continue to practice a form of Buddhist meditation; others find Taoist and Confucian insights helpful and wonder whether Christianity could supplement or enhance their hunger for spirituality.

These hopeful wallflowers come to the dance representing a broad array of backgrounds and perspectives, but they all share a particular posture toward religious traditions. This posture may not be entirely new in the history of Christianity, but it has appeared in Western societies more explicitly in recent years. Hopeful wallflowers are responding to the energies of human desire, but they're not entirely sure religious faith can satisfy that desire. These wallflowers are not diehard atheists or the merely incredulous, the ones who find religious faith without any merit. Rather, they represent those who want to live with religious faith but refuse to accept religion at face value. The combination of desire and reluctance is what that makes these wallflowers hopeful.

A variety of historical and cultural issues have contributed to the appearance of hopeful wallflowers at the dance. Mostly, they worry about how often Christians stumble on the dance floor. Christians behaving badly throughout history raises doubts about Christianity itself. If, as these wallflowers insist, we can discern something about Christian theology by observing how people put it into practice, then there must be something seriously wrong with Christian theology. The historical proliferation of Christian churches doesn't seem to have made the world any less violent, any less fraught with hostility, any less burdened by the mechanisms of poverty and oppression. In some cases, Christians themselves and Christian theological ideas have exacerbated those problems. When considering twenty-first-century prospects for the dance of faith, some of the more obvious examples of stumbling on the dance floor deserve further attention in the kind of conversations I hope this book will provoke and inspire.

STUMBLING ON THE DANCE FLOOR

The Bible remains a source of perplexity and controversy for many of today's hopeful wallflowers. Christians tend to trip over this collection of texts whenever we try to make something more of it than even the writers of those texts envisioned. Treating scripture either as a religious textbook on science or as speech dictated directly from God inevitably leads to significant stumbling in the dance. At best, those stumbles are simply embarrassing (like the condemnation of what Galileo observed through a telescope); at worst, they lead to social oppression (like supporting slavery). Today, hopeful wallflowers want to know how to read the Bible intelligently while still treating it reverently and explore what kind of role those ancient texts ought to play in a world of empirical science. Does Christian faith really demand we believe Moses encountered a burning bush on a desert mountaintop or that the Red Sea parted just as filmmaker Cecil B. DeMille portrayed it in *The Ten Commandments*? Must Christians reject evolutionary biology and astrophysics in order to believe in God the Creator? How much of the gospels do we assign to a mythological worldview modern people no longer share with those writers? What does it really mean to treat biblical texts as "authoritative"?

Questions such as these prompt broader concerns about the traditional approach to Divine Reality often referred to as classical theism. The word "God" is still tightly bound up with these classic Western notions of an all-powerful, all-knowing father figure. Hopeful wallflowers will want to talk about how these notions differ—if at all—from what Dorothy discovered in *The Wizard of Oz*. Does Christian faith mean believing in the all-powerful "Wizard" while paying no attention to "that man behind the curtain"? These are by no means flippant concerns when Christians struggle with knowing how to pray. We Christians frequently stumble in our prayerful dancing whenever we treat God as a cosmic version of Santa Claus, granting wishes to the well behaved and punishing the naughty. That kind of stumbling simply begs the question of whether the whole notion of God is merely a projection of the human longing for "daddy" to solve our problems.

Christian traditions are not silent on these questions, but the way they have been addressed and who has addressed them can turn out to be just as troubling as the questions themselves. Hopeful wallflowers are quick to notice that historical Christian traditions have been shaped almost exclusively by men and with patriarchal paradigms of reality. Contrary to popular portrayals, feminist critiques of male-dominated religious traditions do not pit men against women; instead, they highlight how patriarchy actively excludes women and women's lives by assuming men and men's lives can adequately represent human experience. Even a cursory reading of early Christian traditions reveals something even more insidious, as many of those texts identify women and the "feminine" generally as representing the very problem Christian faith seeks to solve. As Christians have and continue to stumble over gender on the dance floor, hopeful wallflowers become quite nervous. They begin to wonder whether Christianity remains a viable option for both men and women who seek to end sexist abuse and commit themselves to the full flourishing of women.

Seeking the full flourishing of all people raises additional questions about environmental crises and ecological degradation. Modern industrial societies now pose threats to environmental health in ways ancient Christian theologians could not have imagined. But there is more to worry about on this front when Christian traditions seem to thwart contemporary efforts toward ecological sustainability. Christians continue to stumble, for example, over biblical visions of a "new heaven and a new earth" of the kind found in the Revelation to John (21:1). At best, these visions could promote ecological apathy; at worst, they make this present earth quite literally disposable while we wait for a new one. Hopeful wallflowers worry that such stumbling keeps Christians so heavenly minded that we're no earthly good.[1]

Christian traditions exhibit a rather strange mix between appreciating the goodness of God's creation and treating this planet as deeply flawed and only a temporary rest stop on our way to someplace else. Christian theology never fully resolves that tension, leading some of today's wallflowers to wonder about the relationship between this world and the "world to come." They do more than wonder about that relationship when Christian churches stumble over it and spend more energy on preparing people for heaven than on fostering human thriving now, on Earth. These are some of the concerns theologians consider in the theological subspecialty called eschatology, which comes from the Greek word for "last things." This branch of theology deals with the mysteries of life after death, the Second Coming of Christ, the final judgment, and all those perplexing biblical visions of the Apocalypse. Apocalyptic images of the end of the world are easily caricatured (as they are in many Hollywood films) but not easily ignored. They can also carry profound practical consequences.

In the nineteenth century, Napoleon Bonaparte gave articulate expression to some of the problems with apocalyptic forms of Christianity and why today's hopeful wallflowers tend to worry about it. Reflecting on the social inequities from which he benefited, Napoleon asked: "What is it that makes the poor man take it for granted that ten chimneys smoke in my palace while he dies of cold—that on my table at each meal there is enough to sustain his family for a week? It is religion which says to him that in another life I shall be his equal, indeed that he has a better chance of being there than I have."[2] More than a few wallflowers recognize the continuing challenge posed to Christian faith by Napoleon's astute grasp of theology's practical consequences. They look with dismay at how often Christians have

stumbled over apocalyptic speculation, which has frequently led to supporting rather than critiquing oppressive social structures and cultural institutions that perpetuate poverty and injustice.

All of these complex questions and issues—from how to read the Bible
to the problems with classical theism and the patriarchal imprint of
Christian traditions—have contributed to the appearance of hopeful wallflowers at the Christian dance. They remain hopeful about the potential in
Christian faith and theology but wary, concerned about how often
Christians have tripped over their own theology and stumbled on the dance
floor. For many of these wallflowers, the legacy of apocalyptic traditions
points to and summarizes all of the other problems with which they struggle, and it continues to feed their reluctance to join the dance. Apocalyptic
warnings about the world's end threaten to make Christianity both incredi-
ble and impractical in the struggle for human flourishing.

Anglican Christians rarely succumb to apocalyptic fervor, but we don't
quite know how to address that fervor's persistence in historical and contemporary Christianity. Actually, Anglican traditions are a bit more apocalyptic
than most Anglicans realize. Apart from their potential abuse, apocalyptic
traditions can inspire critical questions about what it means to speak of
divine revelation, whether human history has any discernible purpose, what
Christian hope looks like, and how such hope is put into practice. For the
sake of the wallflowers and for lifelong Anglican dancers, for the sake of the
dance itself, apocalyptic traditions deserve further attention. Rather than
abandoning those traditions or adopting them uncritically, embracing the
eschatological character of Christian faith can suggest fruitful prospects for
a twenty-first-century dance, especially now, as the world of modernity
might well be ending in what some have called the "postmodern" condition.

APOCALYPTIC CHOREOGRAPHY

Historically, in both Jewish and Christian traditions, apocalyptic texts usually appear at times of crisis or of impending crisis in a community's life. In
the Hebrew Bible, the prophet Ezekiel wrote during a time when the
Babylonian army had invaded Israel and marched the Israelites into exile.
The Revelation to John in the Christian scriptures was likely written during a period of severe persecution by the Roman Empire. Those kinds of
apocalyptic texts frequently include dense metaphorical language, visionary

experiences, and complex allegorical references. While the images and historical points of contact vary from text to text, each one has the same purpose: to offer comfort to a community under threat or whose members are suffering.

Apocalyptic texts and traditions offer comfort by placing a given community's life in the context of a much larger, often cosmic story. Rather than depicting it as merely random or meaningless, the community's present crisis is shown as belonging to a still unfolding drama, the final chapter of which will bring the crisis to a meaningful and even joyous resolution. In this way, apocalyptic writers try to counter despair with the confidence that history's final resolution rests in God's hands, not ours.

Throughout Christian history, however, these apocalyptic texts have inspired more than a reasonable hope. The fantastical images, mythological creatures, and cosmic scope of these texts have tempted Christian communities to treat them as blueprints for the future. This temptation is often rooted in a misunderstanding of prophecy, which many people assume is synonymous with prediction. But biblical prophets generally care more about speaking the truth in the present than predicting the precise course of distant events. Even the Revelation to John begins with a series of exhortations addressed to particular historical communities, to churches scattered throughout the Roman Empire. That writer's concern is clearly for the situation those communities were confronting then and there, not whether they could decipher precisely his visions of a far-off future. Nevertheless, the poetic language and mysteriously veiled historical references in apocalyptic texts continue to invite futuristic speculation. They can also generate quite a peculiar way of life.

Many of the Christian scriptures, and not just the Revelation to John, contain traces of apocalyptic or more broadly eschatological sensibilities. Many of those texts, for example, were written with the assumption that Jesus would return very soon, or at least in the writer's own lifetime. Christians in Thessalonica, to whom Paul wrote at least two letters, were perplexed by the death of some their companions, precisely because they believed Christ would return before they had to confront their own mortality (1 Thessalonians 4:13–18). Believing the world sits on the brink of radical transformation also configures a community's common life with a peculiar apocalyptic choreography. The kind of economics practiced by early Christian communities (Acts 4:32–37) and some of the rather odd postures they adopted toward marriage and sexuality, illustrated by Paul's preference for remaining single (1 Corinthians 7), are just two examples. If Christ is coming back soon, there's no point in holding on to private property, and raising a family seems quite beside the point.

These early patterns of Christian life changed significantly as Christians began to revise their assumptions about the Second Coming. Rather than the relatively loose communal structure described in the Acts of the Apostles, Christians began to pay more attention to institutional forms and clerical offices (1 Timothy 3:1–13). The difference between these early and later patterns is similar to the difference between moving to a new city for a temporary job assignment and moving there for a permanent position. If I know I'm going to be living somewhere for only a short time, I'll probably rent an apartment rather than buy a house and I won't pay much attention to local politics. All of that changes when I know I'm going to settle into a place for the long haul—the housing market takes on added significance and who sits on the city council matters as much as who runs for governor.

In the first few centuries of the Christian era, Christian communities began to realize the importance of settling in for the long haul, especially after Constantine's declaration of Christianity as the official religion of the Roman Empire. But the tantalizing energy of apocalyptic traditions continued to percolate, even in the midst of stable institutional structures. Occasionally, this energy boiled over in renewed speculation about the world's end.

In the sixteenth century, for example, Martin Luther was at first deeply reluctant to address the mysterious visions contained in the Revelation to John. Over time, however, when his conflict with the Pope began to escalate, Luther found that biblical text rhetorically useful. The Pope, Luther claimed, was clearly the Antichrist described by John. Some of Luther's contemporaries even began to refer to him as the "Angel of the Apocalypse" who signaled the end of the world. In some ways, of course, they were quite correct. The tightly structured world of medieval Christendom was unraveling and did indeed come to an end in the Protestant Reformation.

Similar moments are sprinkled throughout Christian history when apocalyptic images seem to resonate with current events. The possibility that one's own time and place sits on the brink of the decisive moment in world history continues to fascinate and provoke speculation. When tyrannical dictators resemble the Antichrist and modern military strategies fit the biblical description of the Battle of Armageddon, some Christians naturally wonder whether they shall soon witness the Second Coming and the end of the world.[3]

Actually, all sorts of "worlds" come to an end quite regularly. Roughly seventy years after Jesus was born, the Roman Empire came down brutally on Palestine, sacking Jerusalem, destroying the Temple, killing thousands, and scattering many thousands more to the four corners of the wind. The world described in the gospels came to an end and a new world emerged, a world that gave birth to sibling religious traditions called Judaism and Christianity.

Some four hundred years or so after that, under the onslaught of northern European "barbarians" and many years of extraordinarily corrupt government, the Roman Empire itself collapsed, with its provinces falling into chaos and its citizens cowering in fear. The classical world of Greco-Roman culture came to an end and a new world emerged, a world historians used to call the "Dark Ages."

After the medieval world of Christendom ended in the Protestant Reformation, yet another world began to take shape, a world of colonialism and conquest. The appearance of Europeans on the American continent eventually brought the world of native tribes and peoples to an end and a new world, a world marked by the United States, took its place.

Apocalyptic writers are particularly well attuned to the dynamics of ending worlds. At their best, they refrain from mapping those ends precisely and devising detailed calculations for when they will occur. But these writers and the communities who read their texts are frequently tempted to say too much, to go beyond the fact that worlds do sometimes end, and include explanations of how and when they will. Resisting this temptation is what theologians sometimes call "eschatological reserve," or more simply, humility.

We can say quite a lot about Divine Reality and human life and history and the good news of dancing with the God of abundant life. But we can't say or know everything about such things. We can hear the divine music, learn some choreography, and occasionally find ourselves caught up in the dance itself. But these various moments of divine revelation are always filtered through the cultural modes of perception and peculiar perspectives of particular communities. We need to train our ears to hear the music, learn from our stumbles on the dance floor, and recognize our own limits in a dance that is still unfolding.

Scientists know something about this kind of eschatological reserve in their own work. Biologists, physicists, astronomers, and cosmologists keep making discoveries about the world and how it works and holds together. They can say a great deal about the mystery of life and the fabric of the universe, but they can't say everything about such things. At their best, scientists realize that even the most widely accepted scientific theories remain provisional and subject to modification based on new data. An apocalyptic choreography encourages a similarly humble posture in dancing with God and with each other.[4]

The word "apocalypse" comes from a Greek verb that means, simply enough, "to reveal." But this meaning of the word seems a bit out of place in a text like the Revelation to John. If something important had been revealed to that writer, why couldn't he find a less mysterious way to communicate it? If John intended to provide a precise blueprint for the world's end, why is there so much disagreement over how to interpret it? Rather than maps, blueprints, and predictions, apocalyptic traditions offer a more modest and at the same time more hopeful revelation: the faithfulness of God. This is the comfort and the hope communities in crisis need most.

When the turbulence of change and decay threaten to unravel the comfortable contours of my world, what I really want is the hopeful assurance that God will be faithful. Apocalyptic texts offer such assurance by reminding me that the story of life itself is not yet finished and the final chapters have not yet been drafted. That kind of future is hopeful only insofar as I can trust that what God intends and what God has begun God will indeed accomplish, because God is faithful. How and when God will accomplish what God intends is not for any of us to know, which is why Christian faith is a matter of hope rather than of certainty. In his most apocalyptic moments, even Jesus resorts to that kind of eschatological reserve. After warning his disciples to pay attention to signs and portents in both the skies above and history below as signals of the world's end, Jesus then says, "But about that day or hour no one knows, neither the angels in heaven, nor the Son, but only the Father" (Mark 13:32).

Traces of this humble reserve appear in various religious traditions, whether Christianity, Judaism, or Islam. The mystics and ecstatics in each of these traditions continually remind us of the limits of human knowledge precisely because those limits energize hope. We cannot possibly know where and when one world ends and another begins. We can only trust in the faithfulness of the One who holds all worlds in their living and their dying and gathers them together in an incomprehensible dance. We cannot possibly give adequate voice to that mystery. But we can try, and in our attempts to do so, trust the Spirit to lead us ever deeper into the dance. There, the very idea of a "world" no longer matters when we are caught up in the life of the One who was, who is, and who is to come, the Alpha and the Omega, the beginning and the end and the beginning again.

With these insights in view, Anglican Christianity reverberates with apocalyptic hope. By resisting the temptation to say more than we can know and living with a variety of theological perspectives, even in a single congregation, Anglican Christians bear witness to a faithful eschatological reserve. This does not mean such reserve feels comfortable or that it creates seamless, harmonious communities. And it will mean stumbling on the dance floor quite regularly. Many Anglican Christians disagree about how much we can know theologically and when we have tried to say too much when we speak. These disagreements can lead to vigorous debate and sometimes to the threat of schism. Perpetual revision of liturgical language, to which the many versions of the Prayer Book attest, is a common source of this eschatological discomfort among Anglicans. How we worship and pray together seems inherently unstable, tempting some to call for more liturgical uniformity and for a more decisive theological system.

Embracing an apocalyptic choreography for the dance, and all the restless energy that comes with it, serves as a reminder of the eschatological orientation of Christian faith itself. Throughout church history, whenever Christian communities have settled in to a comfortable pattern of faith and practice, mystical and apocalyptic writers have disrupted that pattern with unsettling visions. These visions and texts rarely blend easily with established theological assumptions, reminding us that Divine Reality continually inspires much more than we can know or say.[5]

Dancing apocalyptically does not, on the other hand, simply invite chaos, nor does it erase the theological traditions of previous generations. Rather, eschatological sensibilities keep those traditions fresh and lively by orienting them toward an unmapped future. Professional dancers know that each new performance holds the possibility of surprise depending on the energy of the audience, the idiosyncrasies of the other dancers, and the condition of their own bodies. Expecting these many variables in any given performance does not make rigorous practice irrelevant. To the contrary, professional dancers continually study and review the basic skills of the dance, trusting that such discipline will prepare them for what they cannot yet anticipate.

Christian theology provides the basic skills we need to step foot on the dance floor of faith and start dancing. But theology cannot tell us about everything we'll experience when we do. The eschatological character of Christian faith orients us toward the edges of the dance floor, which keep receding ever farther from view and inviting us to explore uncharted territory with creativity and innovation. The courage for such exploration comes from the restless energy of hope fueled by apocalyptic visions of a world that is not yet finished, the choreography of which we have only just begun to learn.

Anglican Christianity tries to embrace this hopeful restlessness in the ongoing process of conversation and conversion in which one's own insights and skills are never quite sufficient. This process involves retrieving insights from historical traditions, bringing them into conversation with the present, and expecting new steps for the dance will emerge as our lives and our institutions undergo continual conversion. We cannot predict the shape of those evolutionary turns on the dance floor any more than a Pharisee by the name of Saul could have predicted the course of his life as the Apostle Paul. Even after his dramatic moment of conversion, Paul infused his own theology with eschatological reserve. To the Christians in Corinth, Paul insisted that love will last even when all else fades away. Meanwhile, he writes, "we see in a mirror, dimly, but then we will see face to face. Now I know only in part; then I will know fully, even as I have been fully known" (1 Corinthians 13:12).

We may not be able to see clearly now or rely on precise predictions for the future. But we can rely on hope, trusting in the divine faithfulness to which Christian theology tries to point. As Anglicans give voice to that kind of faithfulness, the apocalyptic reluctance to say too much can offer hopeful prospects for a twenty-first-century dance. A faithful eschatological reserve in Anglican Christianity might prove especially helpful for some of the wall-flowers at the dance, the ones who wonder about the tones and rhythms of today's postmodern sensibilities.

POSTMODERN MUSIC

There are nearly as many ways to describe postmodernism as there are writers and scholars who use the term. The difficulty in defining this concept clearly actually reflects one of the features of contemporary Western societies that postmodern thinkers want to describe. We have arrived at a

time in the history of Western ideas and culture in which categorical definitions no longer deliver what they once promised. Modern categories
described the world with precision, whether in terms of race and ethnicity,
or gender and sexuality, or politics and economics. Modern categories
labeled books clearly as either fact or fiction; historians wrote one kind of
book and novelists another. Modern science dispelled myths, whether with
the tools of biology and astronomy or with those of psychology and sociology. Today, the lines between these neatly crafted categories have blurred.
Perhaps they were never as clear as any of us thought, but now the blurring
is impossible to ignore. Now, supposedly self-evident truths are firmly
rooted in particular and therefore variable cultural assumptions. The idea of
any truth being "self-evident" ignores the extent to which human perceptions of reality are always molded by the cultural context in which each of
us lives. Even the idea of truth itself seems murky.

Religious truth falls under the same kind of scrutiny in postmodern circles. The kind of religious worldview I grew up with gave me a way to make
sense of the world, a unified story of human and divine life with a clearly
defined beginning, middle, and end. Believing in a God who creates all that
is, who saves from sin and death, and who sanctifies the faithful were the
self-evident truths of that worldview, the "givens" of my faith. For some time
now, Christian churches have been living with a growing unease about these
and many other "givens" in modern Christianity. Archaeological discoveries,
new historical research, the perspectives of feminist and liberation theologians, and ongoing institutional scandals all call some of the most cherished
Christian "givens" into question. For many postmodern thinkers, even the
idea of "God" seems dubious, mired in so many layers of cultural and historical assumption that the word no longer holds much meaning. Christians
experience some of these postmodern sensibilities whenever they realize that
the Bible doesn't really say what they thought it did, or that it says more than
they expected, or that Christian theology hasn't always articulated what they
grew up believing, or that the religious story they inherited for understanding the world and making sense of it actually leaves out many more pieces
than it includes. The tightly organized world of modern religious faith turns
out to be quite untidy and has more loose ends than any of us knows how
to tie up. From this perspective, the "post" of postmodernism doesn't simply
refer to what "comes next" in Western culture and religion; it refers instead
to not having any clear idea of what ought to or what will come next.

Postmodern music poses some vexing questions, not the least of which is whether anyone can really dance to it. In at least one respect, Anglican Christians have been trying to dance to similar music for a long time and began doing so well before the term postmodernism was coined. As apocalyptic traditions remind us, all sorts of worlds come to an end quite regularly, and it could well be the case that the world of modernity has run its course. What comes next, however, matters far less than living in such apocalyptic moments with hope.

Anglican Christians already know something about such moments, as do many other Christians who trace their historical roots to the Protestant Reformation. For sixteenth-century Europeans, the unraveling of medieval Christendom occasioned just as much daunting and exhilarating reflection as the postmodern scrutiny of modern Christianity does for us. In response, English reformers tried to carve out a rather peculiar kind of religious space, the shape of which might make today's postmodern music a bit less unnerving when we hear it on the dance floor.

Christians in the English Reformation both embraced and resisted the collapse of religion's unifying story represented by Catholicism. While some made vigorous arguments for retaining a Catholic identity apart from its Roman expression, others argued just as vigorously for purifying the Church of England of anything resembling Catholic tradition. Advocates on both sides were venturing into unknown territory without Rome and without having a clear vision of what would come next. As these innovative Anglicans reached a compromise in the Elizabethan Settlement, the *via media* it produced was not merely a convenient stopgap measure born from political expediency (even if it was at least that much). An Anglican *via media* doesn't shore up religion's crumbling walls, but it doesn't tear them down, either. In fact, that kind of substantive metaphor misses the point entirely.

Religious faith is not a place or a thing and certainly not a fortress in need of protection. As the Anglican concept of *via media* implies, Christian faith invites a sense of movement and travel, a way forward that rests neither here nor there but journeys through the mysterious space in between. The image of traveling is not necessarily unique to Anglicans, but the *via media* does offer a particular way to make the journey.

As with any journey, those who embark on the journey of faith need supplies, and there are many from which to choose: the texts of scripture, centuries of theological reflection, liturgies, hymns, philosophy, literature, the human and physical sciences, art and culture. The list of possible supplies grows longer every day, especially in an age of global communication when insights from other religious traditions and non-Western cultures are added to the list. Discerning suitable supplies for the journey and anticipating what the journey will require along the way requires critical and sustained reflection among faithful travelers. Whenever I travel, even for just a long weekend, I tend to overpack and find myself encumbered by things I didn't really need. I hardly ever realize it until I'm actually on the road. An Anglican *via media* invites a similar scrutiny of theological baggage.

Since the sixteenth century, Anglican Christians have at times paused on the journey to reevaluate the supplies we're carrying with us to determine whether some are no longer needed and whether some new ones would be useful for the road ahead. At one such moment, Anglicans decided that the doctrine of purgatory was just a bit too heavy and could be safely discarded. Those same Anglicans, however, retained the traditional pattern of church polity that included bishops and dioceses, even though they created ample space for periodic reassessments of what kind of authority bishops ought to exercise. Church conventions and synods engage in similar moments of scrutiny all the time as the many resolutions, the process of debate, and political maneuverings offer an opportunity to examine and catalogue our religious luggage. This can often be quite messy. The next time you hear about or attend a church convention, imagine a train stopped at a station and the station platform littered with open suitcases as passengers try to discern what they need for the next leg of the journey.

Dancing well involves a similar process. After traveling around the dance floor for a while, every dancer needs to take a break and return to the dance studio for some evaluation and reflection. The costume might need some adjustment to allow freer movement; a particular turn or step might have felt clumsy in practice and requires some innovation; additional creativity is needed in coordinating the choreography to allow a bit more space among the dancers. Taking time for disciplined reflection in the dance studio can equip dancers with critically important skills, but it can't anticipate every step they will need to take when they rejoin the dance. As Anglican Christians continually discover, dancing along the *via media* requires a rather high tolerance for ambiguity, the willingness to encounter occasionally arcane religious customs, and the fortitude to engage in frequent disagreements without the assurance of definitive resolution.

Reflecting on the history of an Anglican *via media* offers a way to dance to some of the postmodern music playing on the dance floor today and suggests prospects for how the dance will continue to unfold. Such prospects will lead as surely into the realm of artists as they do into the world of textual interpreters; as decisively into the language of poets as into the linear prose of an argument; and as compellingly into discovering beauty as in discerning truth. Rather than problems to solve, postmodern sensibilities present an unfinished world of maps yet to be drawn, horizons still unexplored, and more music left to play than we had imagined for a dance that has only just begun. Some of the standard supplies for the dance are still quite useful; some need to be discarded; some new ones will need to be found.[6]

I don't mean to suggest that the many tones and rhythms of postmodern music should sound familiar to Anglicans or to anyone else, or that such music is easy to choreograph. To the contrary, postmodern cadences perpetually disrupt the melodies with which modern Western societies are most familiar and can sound rather jarring, like unexpected, discordant notes. Ignoring those disruptions by resorting to modern versions of religious harmony simply fails to account for the depth of cultural and religious differences in the worldwide human family. Anglican Christians confronted similarly perplexing issues in the potentially explosive diversity of sixteenth-century England, to which they responded with what amounts to a tenuous truce. The religious space created by this truce allowed them to trust that the dance would unfold as God intends even while they fiddled with the choreography. Many of them no doubt assumed the dance would disclose a much more definitive shape by now; of course, it hasn't. The dance of Christian faith in Anglican contexts has continued to whirl into some surprising patterns and movements. Today, Anglicans face the task of carrying that sixteenth-century "truce" into a world of global multiculturalism, the shape of which Anglican pioneers like Thomas Cranmer and Richard Hooker could not have dreamed. Yet the hope they practiced still offers important insights for us, but only if we can learn from encounters with diversity rather than treating those encounters as problems in need of a solution.

The process of learning from diversity depends on a posture of welcome. This process can begin quite simply, as it did for me when I realized that the particular Jesus of the Gospels bore only a slight resemblance to the Jesus I had constructed from the cultural patterns and paradigms of the American Midwest. That one realization led me to consider more carefully the limited scope of my own theological convictions. If even Jesus appears not only as companion and friend but also and just as potently as stranger and "other," modern notions of "self-evident truth" start to weaken and eventually collapse under the weight of countless layers of cultural assumptions. Embracing the "otherness" of Jesus as both insightful and life giving can urge a similar posture toward all the other encounters with otherness on the journey. Rather than merely tolerating diversity, which often means little more than "putting up" with it, this posture of embrace takes seriously the root meaning of the word "welcome." This means, at the very least, saying to the stranger and radically other, it is *well* that you have *come* into my life; you are indeed *welcome*, because I must learn from you.

Learning from the other dramatically recasts modern notions of individual self-sufficiency and modern projects of self-actualization. Whatever else we wish to retain from the historical rhythms of Trinitarian Christian faith, those rhythms would surely assist us in projects of social- and not merely self-actualization. As the vast web of planetary connections comes into view in clearer ways every day, human thriving demands more intentional and creative projects of social engagement. Today's global landscape is too complex, too richly textured, too shot through with moments of wonder and mystery to suppose we can interact with it adequately with just one set of tools, with just one sketch of reality, with just one method of reflection; an individual's limited scope of vision proves woefully inadequate. We need not lament such limitations as an accident or the tragic result of humanity's fall from innocence into sin; as Christian traditions suggest, those limitations are part and parcel of the divine design of reality.

Struggling with the truly arduous and necessarily social dance of conversation and conversion is one of the key ways to hear the music planted in us by the Divine Composer. The world a Trinitarian God creates does not make truth obvious or self-evident to individuals or even to a single culture or group. Instead, the ancient touchstones of Goodness, Truth, and Beauty must be sought after, discerned, and articulated in the company of others. A Trinitarian world demands teams of investigators, whose insights are reflected upon by communities of thinkers, spoken only by a chorus of voices, and then choreographed into a genuinely communal dance, the contours of which we have only begun to glimpse.

The undeniably hard work a communal engagement with the world requires can tempt us to wonder whether God could have found a better way to help us dance, something a bit less fraught with periodic irruptions of hostility and tragic misunderstandings. Perhaps God could have, but then we might well have missed out on the adventure God invites us to take. The adventure begins with the realization that my own limited perspective will not suffice for the journey. I need encounters with the stranger, the alien Other. You and I were created with this need for the Other, not because God is a hard taskmaster but because God is love. If I did not fundamentally need encounters with diversity, I would have no need of you or anyone else and I would never learn the lessons of humility, the art of communication and intimacy, and would never embark on that adventure of vulnerability and trust in which I discover the joy of giving myself away in love.

Anglican Christians offer a fruitful method for shaping that adventure today. The tools for that method, the tools of scripture, tradition, and human experience, have been present in Christian traditions for many centuries. But using those tools in a particularly Anglican way started to take shape when Henry VIII severed his ties with Rome: sustaining genuine conversation; acknowledging human fallibility; embracing a liminal identity; and engaging in common prayer. Today, postmodern music urges a more intentional and creative deployment of that Anglican *via media*, especially in encounters with diversity, with the strangers and alien others encountered on the dance floor. Welcoming the insights from those encounters might also prove helpful for the many wallflowers at the dance, still wary of religious choreography but hopeful nonetheless. From the very beginning, biblical writers recognized the importance of these strange encounters, especially in their accounts of resurrection.

The Gospels share at least this much in common about the risen Jesus: God-in-Christ comes to us first not as familiar friend but as peculiar stranger, the alien other. Luke's gospel, for example, describes the aftermath of crucifixion, those devastating days when so much energy and time spent on envisioning a new world seemed entirely for naught. In those days, as Luke tells it, two disciples were walking along a road to a village called Emmaus. Along the way they encountered a stranger, someone they didn't recognize and whom they assumed they had not met before. And didn't their hearts burn within them, they would later say, when that stranger opened the scriptures to them, when that "alien other" spoke in new and challenging ways about their life and their pain and their fear? And were they not compelled, perhaps for reasons beyond their own comprehension, to invite this stranger to stay with them once they arrived in Emmaus and to share a meal together? It was then, according to Luke, when the bread was broken in the meal they shared, that those disciples finally recognized this stranger from whom they had learned so much. He was none other than the one whose death they had been mourning on the road. And in that very moment of recognition, Jesus disappears (Luke 24:13–35).

Christian life has always resembled that journey on the road to Emmaus, but perhaps especially so today. The disciples' perplexity over current events sounds quite familiar. Their experience of grief and regret and the burden of betrayal they carried could easily describe the dynamics of countless relationships and communities today. Like those disciples, many of us find biblical texts confusing, or at least not as clear as we once thought. The old familiar story now includes a plot twist, making us wonder where to place our trust. The music has suddenly changed, right in the middle of the dance, and the steps feel quite strange. Some guidance would be helpful, but in times of uncertainty and fear, most of us are deeply reluctant to listen to strangers. And just like those disciples, even when we do have the courage to listen and insights start to emerge, those insights vanish as quickly as they appear.

Presumably, Luke offered the Emmaus road story as an account of good news and to inspire hope. If so, then Christian faith cannot rely only on its many texts and traditions. Christian faith is good news when all those words and concepts give us the courage to venture out on the road where there is still much more to learn, even from the most familiar story. Christian faith is hopeful when it welcomes the new insights discovered on the road and expects to discover even more over the horizon. As Paul reminded the Romans, Christians hope for what cannot yet be seen; the restless energy of that hope keeps us focused on the road ahead.

Paul's letter to the Romans and Luke's Emmaus road story are reminders of the unfinished character of Christian theology. The many centuries of Christian ideas and practice can only point to those dynamic encounters with Divine Reality when God comes to meet us in unexpected ways. Traveling on such a road of surprising encounters can feel exciting and frightening at the same time, which makes traveling with companions so important. Christianity offers many companions for the journey, both historical and contemporary, whose company can help dispel anxiety and fear. While those companions provide a great deal, they can't tell us exactly what we'll discover on the road ahead. They can, however, remind us that God will be faithful. Regardless of what happens on the road and over the horizon, God will be faithful. This is surely one of the most important things we can learn from the history of Christian traditions: No matter how often we stumble, God will not, because God is faithful. Letting those reminders of divine faithfulness sink into our bones and muscles turns our traveling into dancing.

Luke also suggests something a bit more concrete to do in the meantime, in times of uncertainty and perplexing diversity, in times when the hope of human flourishing seems threatened by fear and despair. In such mean times, Luke suggests sharing a meal. Anglican Christians have taken that suggestion to heart in the energy we devote to eucharistic liturgy. But Luke's story suggests something further, something particularly appropriate for an age of postmodern music: One of the most faithful things Christians can do is to break bread with strangers. And this, Luke seems to say, is how we begin to practice hope.

~ Notes ~

Introduction: The Priest and the Disc Jockey

1. Former Archbishop of Canterbury Michael Ramsey made a similar observation. Rather than based in systems or confessional statements, Anglican Christianity is primarily a "method, a use, and a direction, it cannot be defined or even perceived as a 'thing in itself,' and it may elude the eyes of those who ask 'What is it?' and 'Where is it?' It has been proved and will be proved again, by its fruits and works." *To Believe Is to Pray: Readings from Michael Ramsey*, ed. James E. Griffiss (Cambridge: Cowley Publications, 1996), 44.

2. Some Anglicans have tried to make a system from Thomas Cranmer's liturgical theology, but historical theologian Henry Chadwick cautions against this view: "Anglicans have never thought of Thomas Cranmer as the author of a systematic theology retaining normative value for succeeding generations. . . . There has been no time in Anglican history when a controversy could be settled by some apt quotation from Cranmer's works." "The Context of Faith and Theology," in *Theology in Anglicanism*, ed. Arthur Vogel (Wilton, Conn.: Morehouse-Barlow, 1984), 28.

3. Mark McIntosh, *Mystical Theology: The Integrity of Spirituality and Theology* (Oxford: Blackwell Publishers, 1998), 7.

1. Waltzing the Two-Step: A Hopeful Theological Method

1. In dealing with scripture, tradition, and reason, Arthur Vogel observes, we are not "dealing with three absolutes, three ingredients that stand outside each other and are only externally related." These sources, rather, "penetrate each other" in a tension both "open and dynamic." Preface, *Theology in Anglicanism*, 8.

2. In *The Poetic Imagination: An Anglican Spiritual Tradition* (New York: Orbis, 2000), biblical scholar L. William Countryman makes a similar point. "Spirituality," he notes, "like conversation, is in a constant process of becoming. It is always in motion, as is appropriate to the fact that we are finite creatures. Our humanity is not fully realized or realizable in a single moment, cannot be present even to itself all at once. It is always in the process of becoming" (20).

3. Throughout Christian history, Christian communities have sometimes exercised religious authority coercively, forcing conformity by means of either civil or ecclesiastical power or both. Anglicans have come to appreciate a different view of authority, which also resonates just as well with Christian history: the authority of persuasion. See David S. Cunningham,

These Three Are One: The Practice of Trinitarian Theology (Oxford: Blackwell, 1998), especially how he relates notions of persuasion to Trinitarian doctrine (305–35).

2. The Dance Floor: An Invitation to Courageous Faith

1. John Macquarrie argued for paying a bit more attention to systematic theology among Anglicans, not for the sake of systems themselves but because the complexities of the modern world require more than just an occasional treatise on a particular problem. Theology in Anglican Christianity, Macquarrie writes, has generally dealt only with those matters where Anglicans seem to break with ancient tradition or need to address an issue that ancient thinkers had not considered. Anglicans need not fear systematic theology will "freeze the issues" or inhibit "that theological freedom which is part of the Anglican heritage." "The Anglican Theological Tradition," in *The Anglican Tradition*, ed. Richard Holloway (Wilton, Conn.: Morehouse-Barlow, 1984), 37.

2. Rebecca Lyman's work in historical theology continually reminds us that a single interpretation of the Bible and an unbroken catholic tradition are really historical fictions. "In our desire for unity," she writes, "or in our nostalgia for the past, we may forget that theological diversity is also part of an apostolic church. . . . In spite of the sharp rhetorical categories of orthodoxy and heresy, both negotiation and compromise were also part of historical catholicity in the early church." *Early Christian Traditions* (Cambridge: Cowley, 1999), 163.

3. Hearing the Music: The Trinitarian Rhythms of Christian Faith

1. Many, though certainly not all, concerns about theological language have emerged explicitly from feminist approaches to theology. In *Naming the Mystery: How Our Words Shape Prayer and Belief* (Cambridge: Cowley, 1990), Anglican theologian James E. Griffiss observes how "the critique of Christian language about God and the names which we use for God is not limited to the women's movement in the United States. It also involves how Christians in other cultures will speak about God. We need to see how a particular culture can shape our understanding of God and so also our naming of God. How are we to interpret these names for people to whom they are foreign?" (6–7).

2. Rowan Williams, *A Ray of Darkness: Sermons and Reflections* (Cambridge: Cowley, 1995), 99.

3. L. William Countryman describes Anglicans as suspicious of precise definitions, both for God and for ourselves, in part because of the risk such precision poses to the ineffable mysteries of both divine and human life—"one must not pretend to know too much." *The Poetic Imagination*, 36.

4. As Rebecca Lyman puts it, "diversity is not denied in orthodoxy, but it is disciplined in a particular fashion to ensure transcendent universality and pragmatic unity. To express this unity second-century authors began to use the term 'right belief' (note, not 'same' belief) to distinguish the range of acceptable interpretations which excluded their opponents, now called 'heretics.'" "Natural Resources: Tradition without Orthodoxy," *Anglican Theological Review* 84, no. 1 (Winter 2002): 73.

5. David S. Cunningham makes a similar point by calling on Christian communities to consider Trinitarian doctrine directly in relation to how they live. "One of the reasons that issues of concrete practice engender so much disagreement," he writes, "is that they can only begin to make sense if they are *lived*, rather than merely discussed. Thus, the practices that

I describe [in this book] can only be fully persuasive when one participates in them as a member of the Christian community. Indeed, my goal throughout this book has been to coax trinitarian theology out of its typical surroundings (the ethereal world of verbal abstraction) and into the context of concrete practice." *These Three Are One*, 236.

6. Rosemary Radford Ruether describes theological symbols and formulas as ways to illuminate some aspect of human experience. Institutional structures and systems of authority, however, "try to reverse this relation and make received symbols dictate what can be experienced as well as the interpretation of that which is experienced. In reality, the relation is the opposite." *Sexism and God-Talk: Toward a Feminist Theology* (Boston: Beacon, 1983), 12.

7. Sarah Coakley notices this dynamic with reference to Paul's letter to the Romans—in which she finds hints of later Trinitarian developments—and in the phenomenon of lovers finding the love between them, or their "shared transcendence" as a third element at play in their relationship. See "Living into the Mystery of the Holy Trinity: Trinity, Prayer, and Sexuality," *Anglican Theological Review* 80, no. 2 (Spring 1998): 223–32.

8. William Temple, *Christian Faith and Life* (London: SCM, 1931), 67.

4. Holy Hula Hoops: Jesus and the Hope for Human Thriving

1. The dynamics of race and ethnicity are, of course, much more complex than I have presented here. At the very least, it's important to remember that thinking of humanity as categorically divisible into different "races" appeared around the seventeenth century and quickly developed into a system of classification based on outward appearances (skin color, facial features, etc.) as indicators of inward qualities and values (gentle or violent, inventive or crafty, incisive or capricious, etc.) and that such divisions and categories can hold significant theological and spiritual, not to mention political and economic consequences. See Robert Hood, *Social Teachings in the Episcopal Church* (Harrisburg, Pa.: Morehouse Publishing, 1990), 101–2.

2. Rowan Williams, *Resurrection: Interpreting the Easter Gospel* (London: Darton, Longman & Todd, 1982), 105.

3. Ibid., 101.

4. Rowan Williams, *On Christian Theology* (Oxford: Blackwell, 2000), xiii. The historical construction of orthodoxy and heresy as decisive institutional categories deserves a bit more nuance than my description, or even Williams's approach, would suggest. As Rebecca Lyman reminds us, "orthodoxy" was indeed a weapon used by the powerful against the weak. Moreover, this legacy of restricted speech "is the persistence of our singular, ideological identity, which of course can be used by the right or left who wish to enforce either conformity or diversity." "Natural Resources: Tradition without Orthodoxy," 77.

5. See, for example, Hebrews 9:11–28. Other biblical writers adopt a similar but not identical approach, especially when they employ images like "the lamb of God" to describe Jesus. However, the most explicit attempt to create direct links among the ideas of ancient animal sacrifice, forgiveness, salvation, and the death of Jesus appears in Hebrews.

6. For a succinct overview of these historical issues and their contemporary implications, see Kathryn Tanner, "Incarnation, Cross, and Sacrifice: A Feminist-Inspired Reappraisal," *Anglican Theological Review* 86 (2004): 35–56. Tanner acknowledges, for example, the significance of the cross in the early theological construe of the struggle against sin and death. But these same theologians understood that "the incarnation is the very means by which the fight is waged and won. . . . All of them view the incarnation, understood as the Word's

assumption of humanity—the Word uniting humanity to itself in such a way as to make humanity its own—as the key to the salvation of humanity" (41).

7. John L. Kater Jr., *Finding Our Way: American Christians in Search of the City of God* (Cambridge: Cowley, 1991), 122.

8. William Temple, *Nature, Man and God* (London: Macmillan, 1934), 478.

5. The Tango: A Spirituality of Divine Seduction

1. Hans Frei, *Theology and Narrative: Selected Essays*, ed. George Hunsinger and William C. Placher (Oxford: Oxford University Press, 1993), 162.

2. Rowan Williams, *Resurrection*, 52.

3. Rowan Williams, "The Body's Grace," in *Our Selves, Our Souls and Bodies: Sexuality in the Household of God*, ed. Charles Hefling (Cambridge: Cowley, 1996), 59.

4. Annie Dillard, *Teaching a Stone to Talk: Expeditions and Encounters* (New York: Harper & Row, 1982), 41.

6. The Virginia Reel: Visions of Unrealized Communion

1. Njongonkulu Ndungane, "Scripture: What Is at Issue in Anglicanism Today?" *Anglican Theological Review* 83, no. 1 (2001): 18.

2. Ibid., 20.

3. Temple himself recognized the shortcomings of his own approach. He continued to insist on the church's "right" to intervene in matters of social and economic policy, describing the separation of religion and politics into separate spheres as a "modern aberration." But he eventually modified his more ambitious proposals by acknowledging the limits of the church's competence. See Alan Suggate, *William Temple and Christian Social Ethics Today* (Edinburgh: T & T Clark, 1987), especially chap. 15 in which Suggate outlines the influence of American theologian Reinhold Niebuhr on Temple's later approach.

4. Gardiner H. Shattuck Jr. offers an insightful account of how the Episcopal Church in the United States has addressed issues of racism in *Episcopalians and Race: Civil War to Civil Rights* (Lexington: University of Kentucky Press, 2000). Likewise, Robert E. Hood illustrates the dynamic exchange between institutional texts and cultural practices concerning a variety of issues in *Social Teachings of the Episcopal Church*. In chap. 7, for example, he traces the evolution of the Episcopal Church's theological reflection on economics from early twentieth-century labor movements to the Great Depression and into more contemporary issues and shows how the church's theological texts changed, both in emphasis and content, based on various cultural challenges and problems (163–180).

5. David S. Cunningham reminds us that even John Henry Newman, an Anglican champion of the "high church" perspective who later converted to Roman Catholicism, embraced a dynamic relationship between texts and practices. Newman's work, Cunningham notes, provides "a number of historical examples to show that the body of faithful Christians often kept the truth alive, even when it was in danger of eclipse on the 'official' levels of church teaching." *These Three Are One*, 320.

6. Liturgical theologian Louis Weil makes a similar point: "The celebration of the liturgy is the *work* of the Church; it is the doing of its identity. It is always the action of an assembly of people who gather because what Christian faith impels them to do must, in its most normative expression, be done together." "Worship and Pastoral Care," in *Anglican Theology and Pastoral Care*, ed. James E. Griffiss (Wilton, Conn.: Morehouse-Barlow, 1985), 116.

7. Hymn text by William Harry Turton, in *The Hymnal* 1982 (New York: The Church Hymnal Corporation, 1982), 315.

Prospects for the Dance: Hopeful Wallflowers and Postmodern Anglicans

1. In the 1980s, for example, James Watt, the U.S. Secretary of the Interior, defended the exploitation of natural resources by saying, "I don't know how many future generations we can count on before the Lord returns" (quoted in Catherine Keller, *Apocalypse Now and Then: A Feminist Guide to the End of the World* [Boston: Beacon Press, 1996], 182).

2. Quoted in Alex R. Vidler, *The Church in an Age of Revolution* (New York: Penguin, 1971), 19.

3. In *Arguing the Apocalypse: A Theory of Millennial Rhetoric* (New York: Oxford University Press, 1994), religion scholar Stephen D. O'Leary offers several historical examples of this kind of speculation and the practical consequences it can generate in a community's life, including the apocalyptic imagery that infused the cold war rhetoric of the 1980s (see especially chaps. 6 and 7).

4. Current scientific theories about the universe do more than model humility; they actually suggest several scenarios about how the universe will one day end, whether in cosmic contraction (the reverse of the "big bang") or in gradually life-extinguishing expansion. John Polkinghorne, a scientist and an Anglican theologian, offers a way to integrate contemporary scientific insights about the world with Christian traditions of eschatological hope. See *The God of Hope and the End of the World* (New Haven, Conn.: Yale University Press, 2002), especially chaps. 1 and 2, for an overview of scientific cosmology and chap. 10 for reflection on "the new creation" and the "world to come."

5. Mark McIntosh describes mystical theology as "theology that lets its own speech be questioned and even stripped away by the mystery of God—who can never really become the scientific 'object of study' for theology, but always remains the acting Subject." *Mystical Theology*, 40.

6. Christians need not, nor should we, dance to postmodern music uncritically. Postmodern sensibilities themselves deserve just as much scrutiny as the religious and philosophical traditions they try to critique. Indeed, Mark McIntosh offers some compelling reasons to treat postmodern critiques with suspicion (*Mystical Theology*, 213–19), which simply reminds us even further that the Christian journey demands constant vigilance, requires multiple tools of analysis, and incorporates a wide array of perspectives. Anglican Christians have known this for some time.